THE AUSTRALIAN SHEPHERD

Tracy Libby

The Australian Shepherd

Project Team
Editor: Heather Russell-Revesz
Copy Editor: Joann Woy
Design: Angela Stanford
Series Design: Mada Design and Stephanie Krautheim
Series Originator: Dominique De Vito

T.F.H. Publications
President/CEO: Glen S. Axelrod
Executive Vice President: Mark E. Johnson
Publisher: Christopher T. Reggio
Production Manager: Kathy Bontz

T.F.H. Publications, Inc.
One TFH Plaza
Third and Union Avenues
Neptune City, NJ 07753

Printed and bound in China
08 09 10 11   3 5 7 9 8 6 4
Library of Congress Cataloging-in-Publication Data
Libby, Tracy, 1958-
  The Australian shepherd / Tracy Libby.
     p. cm.
  Includes index.
  ISBN 978-0-7938-3677-2 (alk. paper)
  1. Australian shepherd dog. I. Title.
  SF429.A79L53 2007
  636.737--dc22
  2006101396

This book has been published with the intent to provide accurate and authoritative information in regard to the subject matter within. While every resonable precaution has been taken in preparation of this book, the author and publisher expressly disclaim responsibility for any errors, omissions, or adverse effects arising from the use or application of the information contained herein. The techniques and suggestions are used at the reader's discretion and are not to be considered a substitute for veterinary care. If you suspect a medical problem consult your veterinarian.

The Leader In Responsible Animal Care For Over 50 Years.®
www.tfh.com

TABLE OF CONTENTS

1

HISTORY

of the Australian Shepherd

The Australian Shepherd is a true American success story. Despite his name from the Land Down Under, the modern-day Australian Shepherd we know and love is a product of the good ol' U.S.A. The Aussie, as he is affectionately known, has his feet firmly planted on red, white, and blue soil. He is as American as apple pie and the American West—where he became indispensable to the farmers, ranchers, and shepherds working flocks on the untamed ranges. Despite his American heritage, the Australian Shepherd is a breed with an unclear past. Your Aussie's ancestors were always working dogs—but they were not always Aussies!

Over the years, various theories and a great deal of speculation have been put forth regarding the Australian Shepherd's ancestors and his precise origin. Some suggest that the breed is of Australian origin. Others theorize a Spanish or Basque foundation. These speculations have, naturally, sparked spirited debate. Evidence suggests that separately none of these theories provide the entire story, but together they may help to link important parts of Australian Shepherd history.

It is safe to say that the history and origin of the Australian Shepherd is not a documented record. Much of what we know about the breed is shrouded in mystery, with little or no documentation for verification. What owners and breed historians must rely on has been passed down mostly through nineteenth century legends, personal dairies, photographs, and by word of mouth, from those who knew and loved the breed years before our time.

HERDING DOGS IN HISTORY

Herding dogs have been around for thousands of years, perhaps as many as 14,000 years according to some accounts, but no one knows for certain when they were first trained to earn their keep herding sheep. Biblical references, such as Job 30:1, refer to dogs with flocks. The Roman scholar Marcus Terentius Varro (116–27 B.C.E.) wrote about the care and training of shepherd dogs, and about a sheepdog he procured as a watchdog. Others, including Xenophon, an early pupil of Socrates (430–355 B.C.E.); the Greek philosopher Aristotle (384–322 B.C.E.); and the Greek historian Flavius Arrianus (C.E. 85–150), were a few of the many early writers who also wrote about working dogs. Dr. John Caisus' book *Treatise on Englishe Dogges*, written in 1570, is considered one of the earliest references to working sheepdogs in Britain.

The earliest sheepdogs, in all probability, descended from guard dogs similar to the drover dogs that accompanied the Romans when they invaded Britain in 43 C.E. These large, courageous, and intelligent dogs transported or "drove" livestock to market. A collection of canines of every size, shape, and color, they were utilized for their proficiency at herding livestock as well as protecting the camp from marauders. These dogs were most likely crossed—intentionally or unintentionally—with other dogs, perhaps including the herding spitz-type dogs belonging to the Viking invaders of Britain between the eighth and ninth centuries. Historians theorize that these breedings produced smaller, active, and agile collie-type working dogs whose instincts were shaped over time to suit man's use. The wool industry was essential to the British economy, and it is likely that shepherds valued these active, agile dogs for herding. Over time, shepherds,

Herding dogs have been around for thousands of years.

ranchers, and farmers selectively bred these dogs to suit their particular needs.

THE SHEEP INDUSTRY'S INFLUENCE

Few documents exist to trace the Australian Shepherd's origin. However, by tracing the history of the sheep industry in North America, it is possible to assemble a historical timeline of working dogs, including Australian Shepherds and Australian Shepherd-type dogs.

Prior to the European colonization of the Americas, Spain and England had booming sheep and woolen textile industries, which were the mainstay of their economies. Spain's development of fine-wooled Merino sheep gave her the competitive edge in the wool trade from the thirteenth to the eighteenth centuries, and emigrating Spaniards brought their sheep with them to the New World. During the 1500s and 1600s, explorers, a few of Basque heritage, carried the Spanish banner north from Mexico into what would eventually become Texas, Arizona, California, and New Mexico. And they brought along their flocks.

Sheep introduced into these areas became the foundation for the first commercial sheep industry in what would later become the United States. And, where there are sheep, there are sheepdogs to herd and protect them. Dogs who accompanied Spanish explorers and immigrants were most likely of Spanish origin, and these contributed to the gene pool of working dogs at that time.

EUROPE'S INFLUENCE

Britain, Scotland, Wales, Ireland, and France had scores of different breeds of pastoral dogs during the 1800s and early 1900s, including Scotch Collies, Dorset Blue Shags, Smithfield sheepdogs, Cumberland sheepdogs, Glenwherry Collies, and Harlequin or Welsh Collies. As immigrants began flooding into North America around the turn of the twentieth century, so too did their dogs. Many fine dogs from the British Isles found their way to America.

Scots from the Border country knew the value of a good herding dog and, when they began emigrating to America, they brought with them their working collies. One such notable immigrant was Andrew Little, a Scot who arrived in Caldwell, Idaho in 1894, with his two Scotch Collies. Little became an integral part of the American West by developing the largest sheep operation in Idaho and perhaps in

Transporting Dogs

Transporting dogs across the Atlantic was no small task, considering it was years before the advent of the jet airplanes that whisk us across "the pond" in a matter of hours. The journey by ship would have taken considerably longer and most likely was fraught with great hardship and peril.

Contrary to its name, the Australian Shepherd is an American breed.

the entire nation. At the peak of his operation, Little had hundreds of fully trained dogs working a 7,000-square-mile area on which more than 300,000 sheep ranged. Little's dogs did everything—they herded, guarded, and protected. While they later came to be called Border Collies, a few of them bear a striking resemblance to today's Australian Shepherd.

During this time, dogs were bred for a specific purpose, such as herding or guarding. In the years leading up to the 1900s, specific dog breeds were not as clearly defined as they are today, and much interbreeding of the various strains of herding dogs occurred. Good working dogs were bred to other good working dogs. Pedigrees and physical appearances seldom factored into the equation.

AUSTRALIA'S INFLUENCE

Europeans also immigrated to Australia, bringing with them their working dogs and livestock. For political reasons, merino sheep were imported from France and Saxony (one of Germany's federal states), rather than Spain. The German Coolie or Koolie dog, which was popular with the German settlers in Australia, is similar in appearance and color to the blue merle Australian Shepherd. It's also believed to have descended in part from Welsh sheepdogs that were taken to Australia by Welsh settlers. Like the Koolie, these Welsh dogs bear a strikingly resemblance to early Australian Shepherds. These working dogs, which still exist in Australia, were most likely crossbred, intentionally or unintentionally, with other Australian dogs.

Just as dogs accompanied sheep from New Spain during the 1600s, dogs accompanied sheep imported from Australia to the western United States during the 1940s. Some historians believe these dogs were German Coolies or German Coolie-type dogs, although no one knows for certain. While working on western farms and ranches, these dogs contributed to the general gene pool of working collies/ shepherds, and they may figure prominently in the Australian Shepherd heritage.

THE BASQUE INFLUENCE

Australian Shepherds have always been closely associated with Basque shepherds but, as history reveals, the association may be more by happenstance than design.

Basques were among the first Europeans to emigrate to the New World, with significant numbers settling in the Spanish New World. Many came from a homeland where the western range of the Pyrenees meets the Bay of Biscay, forming part of the border between France and Spain.

In later centuries—the 1830s and 1850s—Basques emigrated to Argentina and the American West. They played a big part in building Andrew Little's Idaho sheep operation, and they comprised much of the work force in sheep outfits in Idaho and other parts of the western

United States. However, unlike the Scots, most Basque immigrants did not bring dogs with them. Most Basques emigrating to America, Argentina, and Australia sought a better life, but not specifically as shepherds. They learned new trades (including shepherding) and, in true Basque tradition, they became masters at whatever trade they tackled.

Like the Scots, Basque shepherds often were paid in land and sheep, and they too began to make their mark on America. Most purchased, traded, or acquired dogs from other Basques, who had earlier emigrated to California, Oregon, Nevada, and Idaho. Some acquired dogs from other ranchers, farmers, or neighbors. Many acquired their dogs from ranchers like Andrew Little, who employed their services.

Australian Shepherds may be descended from German Coolie dogs and Welsh sheepdogs.

The Australian Shepherd Club of America's first conformation show was held at Himmel Park, Tuscon, AZ., April 1958.

In the 1930s, Basques began to emigrate from their homeland to Australia, which also had a booming sheep industry. Although not involved in the Australian sheep industry, Basques began emigrating from Australia to the western United States around 1940—the same time sheep accompanied by dogs were also being imported from Australia. These dogs, which may have been German Coolie-type dogs, resembled blue merle Australian Shepherds.

The Basques were excellent shepherds, and they played an important role in the American sheep industry during the early and mid-1900s—at the same time the Australian Shepherd began to emerge as a breed of its own. It is logical to assume that people would have seen this type of dog with Basque shepherds and assumed they were of Basque origin.

CALIFORNIA'S GOLD RUSH

The number of sheep in the West declined by the end of the 1840s. However, in 1848, the California Gold Rush caused a mass migration of people moving westward to California's gold country in search of an easy fortune. The flood of people created an increased need for mutton and wool for food and clothing. As a result, large flocks of sheep were driven from the Midwest and New Mexico. Dogs accompanying the large flocks were mostly likely old-fashioned Collie-type dogs or shepherd dogs that came to America with settlers from the British Isles.

One of the more popular collie-type dogs being bred on American farms and ranches during this time was the bob-tailed English Shepherd, sometimes called an American Shepherd. In the western United States, similar looking dogs eventually came to be called Australian Shepherds.

Turn of the century photographs show dogs resembling Australian Shepherds posed or working with western homesteaders, ranchers, farmers, and families. Were these farm dogs Australian Shepherds? Most likely, these were old-fashioned collie or shepherd-type dogs, although no one knows for certain. (In hindsight, people often label nineteenth- century dogs with modern breed names, such as Australian Shepherds, but this is not really accurate.)

Today's English Shepherd still looks much like an Australian Shepherd, and many breed historians believe the English Shepherd is an ancestor of today's working Australian Shepherd.

THE MELTING POT

The tremendous influx of immigrants and their dogs to the United States created a melting pot for dogs as well as people. As more and more people immigrated, more and more dogs were included in the general collie/shepherd gene pool. Ranchers and farmers bred their dogs for working ability, and these dogs were bred and crossbred with other good working dogs. As different regions were settled and communities established, different types of herding dogs were developed to suit the particular needs of a region's farmers and ranchers. From this general pool of dogs, different breeds, including the Australian Shepherd, began to emerge. Historians believe the Australian Shepherd is predominantly a product of the collie/shepherd gene pool that traces back to the collie/shepherd dogs of the British Isles—with possibly a pinch of Spanish and Basque influence. While the Australian Shepherd is not an Australian breed, the breed's connection to Australia provided his name.

What historians know for certain is that the Australian Shepherd is an American breed, developed on the farms and ranches of America's rugged and untamed West. His remarkable instinct, intelligence, and loyalty is a result of generations of dogs bred to work cattle, sheep, and other livestock.

Unfortunately, history is seldom absolute and, just as we may never know for certain whether George Washington really cut down that infamous cherry tree, we may never know for certain the true origin of the dog we know and love as the Australian Shepherd.

HOW THE AUSSIE GOT HIS NAME

No one knows for certain how a dog developed in America came to be called an Australian Shepherd. Prior to the 1930s, these "little blue dogs" (referring to their trademark blue merle coats) were called Spanish Shepherds, Pastor Dogs, Bob-Tails, Blues, Heelers, New Mexican Shepherds, and California Shepherds. One account refers to an Aussie-type dog in the California-Nevada area as a "Clinker Collie." Thankfully, that name never caught on!

Paul Sollosy began cowboying back in 1926, working in the heart of

The author's great-grandmother holding an Aussie-type pup circa late 1800s.

11

To early cowboys, Aussies were known as "horse savers."

central California's Santa Barbara County. Today, 95 years old, Sollosy still recalls the blue merle dogs. Back then they were called simply "cowdogs." It wasn't until years later that Sollosy heard them referred to as Australian Shepherds. Sollosy and his cowboy counterparts nicknamed the little blue dogs "horse savers" because central California's rugged ravines were too unstable for a horse's footing. As a result, the cowdogs were sent into the ravines to flush out wayward cows.

A few scattered references are made to "Australian Shepherds" in the 1920s. However, written documentation became more prevalent in the 1940s and 1950s—around the same time that Australia sheep were being imported to the western United States. As with the Spanish sheep brought up from Mexico, dogs would have accompanied the sheep from Australia, too. People seeing "little blue dogs" arriving with boatloads of sheep might have associated the dogs from Australia with similar-looking shepherd dogs in the area, thereby lumping them into the general category of "Australian" shepherds. Many theories and stories abound but, no one knows for certain how a magnificent dog developed in the United States ended up with a name from the Land Down Under.

EARLY AUSTRALIAN SHEPHERDS IN AMERICA

The Australian Shepherd remained a relatively obscure breed until the mid-1950s, concentrated mostly in the western and northwestern areas of the United States. Prior to about 1945, little written documentation about the breed exists, and no selective bloodlines could be clearly identified. A number of early breeders were instrumental in setting the course for the Australian Shepherd, and their dogs became important foundation sires and brood bitches.

These early forefathers of the breed, mostly ranchers and farmers, used their dogs in a working environment, relying on these "little blue dogs" for their livelihood. They selected breeding stock based on the dogs' working ability and physical and mental soundness. Conformity of type and appearance are more modern requirements. As a result, dogs who could not survive the work demands were eliminated from the gene pool. We owe to these early breeders an everlasting debt because without their knowledge, forward thinking, dedication, and intestinal fortitude, the Australian Shepherd we know and love today might have turned out to be a dog of a very different color—literally and figuratively.

BREAKING NEW GROUND

In Arizona, about 20 breed enthusiasts founded the Australian Shepherd Club of America (ASCA) in 1957. Recognition of the Australian Shepherd by the American Kennel Club (AKC) was one of ASCA's original goals. However, that goal was not to be realized for more than 30 years. During the early days, ASCA did not have its own registry, and dogs were registered with the International English

Sisler's Blue Dogs

Jay Sisler of Emmett, Idaho, perhaps more so than anyone else in the breed's history, was instrumental in promoting the Aussie breed and propelling its popularity in the 1950s and 1960s. A talented dog trainer, Sisler had Australian Shepherds before they were known as Australian Shepherds—he called them simply "blue dogs." Traveling throughout the United States and Canada, Sisler performed at rodeo shows and county fairs, entertaining countless spectators and generations of kids with his talented Aussies and their amazing tricks.

Sisler acquired his first dog, Keeno, a red male, around 1939. The dog he called his first "Good dog," Keeno was bred to Blue Star, a blue merle bitch of unknown pedigree purchased at a local livestock auction. This mating produced Sisler's Shorty and his littermate brother, Stubby. Both dogs became two of Sisler's most impressive rodeo trick dogs—jumping rope, standing on their heads, balancing on bars, climbing ladders, and much more. His dogs appeared in several films including Disney's STUB: The Greatest Cowdog in the West and Run Appaloosa, Run.

Sisler's dogs, in addition to promoting interest in the breed, figure prominently in the ancestry of many present-day Aussies. Sisler's Shorty became an important foundation sire, siring many of the breed's most important foundation stock. The influence of Sisler's dogs is immeasurable. Their contributions are seen in today's major bloodlines, and are the foundation of many modern breeding programs.

Shepherd Registry (IESR), also known as the National Stock Dog Registry.

ASCA affiliate clubs began springing up in the western states, including the Australian Shepherd Club of Northern California (1963) and the Mountain State Australian Shepherd Club (1962), which later became the Australian Shepherd Club of Colorado.

In 1966, a California affiliate, the Concord Australian Shepherd Club, was unhappy with the direction ASCA was taking, and they formed a new parent club—the International Australian Shepherd Association (IASA). Their goal was to provide Aussie owners the opportunity to earn obedience titles and seek eventual AKC recognition of the Aussie breed. Both IASA and ASCA eventually established registries; the ASCA in 1971, the IASA in 1972. Aussies were registered with both associations, although ASCA would eventually absorb IASA in the early 1980s and become the official registry of Australian Shepherds.

During the early 1970s, ASCA offered conformation, obedience, and tracking titles. In 1974, members established a Stock Dog program, the first of its kind in the United States.

A breed standard was approved in 1961 and revised in 1963, but it was the 1975 formation of a breed standard committee that put the Australian Shepherd breed on the path to developing and retaining its current breed type. The committee, which included some of the nation's most prominent breeders, stockmen, judges, and veterinarians, had the foresight to put pen to paper, describing and standardizing the ideal Australian Shepherd. After multiple rough drafts and revisions, the general membership approved the breed standard, and it became effective January 1977. This standard has

Where to Register Your Australian Shepherd

Australian Shepherds can be registered with several different registries, and you can choose to register your Aussie with one or more of the registries. The breeder should give you the necessary paperwork to send to the proper registry to register the dog in your name. The Australian Shepherd Club of America (ASCA) is the original parent club and principal registry of the Aussie breed. ASCA awards conformation championships, and agility, obedience, tracking, and stockdog certificates. The American Kennel Club (AKC) and Canadian Kennel Club (CKC) are multibreed registries, meaning they register different breeds including the Australian Shepherd. Both award conformation, obedience, agility, tracking, and herding titles. The United Kennel Club (UKC) recognized the Aussie in 1979, and they too sponsor canine events, including agility, conformation, obedience, field trials, and weight-pull competitions.

The Kennel Club in the United Kingdom recognized the Australian Shepherd in 1994, and the breed is eligible to compete at breed shows and in working activities. In 2006, the breed became eligible for Championship status.

served the Australian Shepherd breed for nearly 30 years. At the time of this writing, a new committee is reviewing the 1977 standard for revisions and clarifications, which, like the original standard, will need general membership approval.

In 1985, a few ASCA members petitioned the board of directors to pursue AKC recognition, but this time the majority of the membership was strongly opposed. They felt "show people" would focus on breeding and judging the Aussie on his looks

AKC recognition allows Aussies to participate in AKC-sponsored sports like obedience.

rather than his herding instinct, thereby undermining the breed's intelligence and natural working ability. They feared that, over time, the Aussie would split into two different breeds—a working breed and a show breed.

Proponents of AKC recognition loved the breed equally, but they felt the breed had more to offer. They stressed that AKC recognition would offer owners another venue for competition. The "little blue dogs" developed on American farms and ranches would retain their natural herding instinct and intelligence.

The United States Australian Shepherd Association (USASA) was eventually formed by a splinter group of fanciers for the sole purpose of seeking AKC recognition. In 1991, the Australian Shepherd was admitted into the AKC's Miscellaneous class, causing quite an uproar with ASCA members. The proverbial line in the sand was drawn. Opponents and proponents took up their positions, while others were caught in the middle. Rumors and accusations flew, egos were bruised, friendships were severed, and when the dust settled, the Aussie was admitted into the Herding group with full competition privileges in 1993.

AKC Parent Club

The United States Australian Shepherd Association (USASA) is the American Kennel Club parent club of the Australian Shepherd breed, meaning that, as an AKC affiliate club, they govern and oversee the Aussie breed under AKC guidelines, and host a complete menu of sanctioned shows including agility, conformation, obedience, tracking, and herding. Unlike ASCA, they do not register Aussies because USASA dogs are registered with the AKC.

CHARACTERISTICS

of the Australian Shepherd

very breed has a blueprint for success. This blueprint is called the *breed standard*, and it describes the perfect or ideal dog to which dedicated breeders aspire. Of course, in the game of conformation (showing), there are no perfect dogs. All dogs have faults—some are just more objectionable or noticeable than others. The best breeders, however, strive to remain true to the original function and purpose of the breed as outlined in the breed standard. Judges also use a breed standard to evaluate the dogs exhibited before them at a show.

To the newcomer, a breed standard may seem nothing more than a cluster of strange-sounding words strung together on a piece of paper. However, it is really an outline of the perfect canine specimen, describing everything from height, weight, color and coat, to angulation of limbs, eye size, color, and shape, and what a dog should look like when he is moving. The Australian Shepherd, like most breeds of dog, was developed for a particular task, and each characteristic of the breed listed in the standard is there for a purpose. His almond-shaped eyes, for example, afford better protection in a working environment. The shape of his feet, his length of body, his scissors bite, and even his coat type are specific breed characteristics that make his life and his job easier, and allow him to perform that job with the greatest amount of efficiency.

DECIPHERING THE STANDARD

Breed standards are simultaneously simplistic and complicated. They are simplistic in that they describe the ideal quality, soundness, and beauty of the ideal Australian Shepherd. What could be simpler? On the other hand, they can be complicated for newcomers and even for a few experienced fanciers because their sometimes-cryptic old-fashioned words and terminology makes them a bit confusing to interpret. In the overall scheme of breed standards, the Australian Shepherd standard is relatively new and straightforward, when compared to sorting through the terminology of 100-year-old Terrier standards.

Breed standards describe the ideal Australian Shepherd.

Originally, people who knew dog breeds best and those who worked their dogs, usually stockmen and horsemen, wrote most of the breed standards because they had extensive knowledge of dogs under working conditions. By simply looking at a dog, these old-timers could say if he was good or not. Therefore, when they wrote a standard, an assumption of dog knowledge and terminology was implied. They did not, for example, waste time writing in a standard that a dog had four legs. They understood *balance* meant "the relationship of one part to another, and of all parts to the whole, in the desired proportions."

They knew *sound* meant free of injury or an absence of lameness. There was no need to spell it out in a standard. As a result, sorting through the terminology and converting word pictures to movement involves a bit of effort, research, and intestinal fortitude on the part of today's fanciers.

That said, once you understand what *clean-cut, dry, and strong* has to do with your Aussie's head, what *firm and clean* mean in relation to his neck, and what the heck they mean by a *four-square* stance—you'll have a better understanding of what the forefathers of the breed were trying to preserve, and what today's breeders strive to replicate.

Why does all this matter to you? Taking the time to learn and understand the breed standard will help you to better understand your Aussie. Why he does what he does, what makes him tick, and why and how each component of your Aussie should work together harmoniously.

STANDARDS OF EXCELLENCE

In the United States, two standards exist for the Australian Shepherd. The Australian Shepherd Club of America (ASCA) breed standard, which was approved in 1977, and for nearly 30 years has served as the breed's official standard, can only be altered or changed by the membership. The Canadian Kennel Club (CKC) and the United Kennel Club (UKC) adopted and adhere to the ASCA standard.

Written in the early 1990s, the American Kennel Club (AKC) breed standard is the second standard. Overseen by the AKC parent club, the

United States Australian Shepherd Association (USASA), and guided by the AKC, it differs slightly from the ASCA standard.

In addition, the Kennel Club in the United Kingdom (KC) controls a British breed standard, which was first published in August 1995.

With the exception of minor variations, the ASCA, AKC, and KC standards describe pretty much the same dog using differing amounts of detailed descriptions and slightly different phraseology.

To help you understand the ASCA, AKC, and KC standards, some important explanations and clarifications are provided in this section.

Breed Type

When you see an Australian Shepherd, you know he is an Australian Shepherd without consciously stopping to think about it. But how? How do you know he is an Aussie and not, say, a Border Collie or a Bernese Mountain Dog. Is it the dog's color? Size? His four-square stance? One is not likely to confuse an Australian Shepherd with a Cardigan Welsh Corgi even though both were originally used as herding dogs. What separates one breed from another are the breeds' individual attributes and characteristics. These attributes and characteristics are called *breed type*—or in canine terminology, the *essence* of the breed. The breed's complete package—the mental and physical characteristics that define what he is, how he looks, how he works, his deportment, and how he conducts himself. In herding breeds, a breed's working style—the method and manner of working livestock— also plays an important part in defining breed type.

Breed type is rooted in a breed's origin—the original purpose and function of a breed. The Australian Shepherd has identifiable characteristics, such as size, proportion, color, markings, and the unmistakable Aussie temperament and personality that were developed and maintained for a specific purpose. These traits have been bred into the breed long enough so that they have become stable, recognizable, reproduced with some uniformity, and

Breed type encompasses the original purpose and function of a breed.

Louis Irigaray spent 31 years as a shepherd, and he captures the essence of working dogs in his book, *A Shepherd Watches, A Shepherd Sings.* "The dogs are workers, employees paid with an evening meal and a pat on the head…. If the sheep are to be dipped in a hole in the ground, bathed in the chemical creosol to kill lice and ticks, five thousand of them headed for a hated swim, canine power sends them out of the corrals and into the tanks. There are no union problems and no other workers on earth are as anxious to get on with the job at hand."

unique to the Australian Shepherd breed. They are the distinguishing features that help you to recognize an Australian Shepherd as being an Australian Shepherd.

Character and Temperament

An important characteristic of the Australian Shepherd is his character and temperament. Think back 100 years to the Australian Shepherd's original purpose and function. He is a product of the American West, where shepherds, farmers, and ranchers needed a sturdy, hard-working, versatile stock dog who could flaunt his intellectual prowess and natural herding ability while working long hours over rugged terrain, in all weathers. A dog who could handle a variety of livestock on the open range and in pens, yet was willing to protect his family and livestock. He needed to be sensitive enough to take direction from his master, yet intelligent enough to make instant decisions and think independently. He needed exceptional athletic ability—to run quickly, change directions without stopping, and spring into immediate action if a sheep or cow were to get out of line. Equally important, he needed to love working with and for his master.

The ASCA breed standard describes the Aussie as being *intelligent, primarily a working dog of strong herding and guardian instincts…versatile, easily trained, performing his assigned tasks with great style and enthusiasm. He is reserved with strangers but does not exhibit shyness. Although an aggressive, authoritative worker, viciousness toward people or animals is intolerable.*

Temperament and working ability go hand-in-hand, and his character and temperament should reflect his original purpose. A dog who has a lot of working ability but an unsuitable temperament—for instance, an independent dog who has little use for human guidance—won't make a good working dog because he will have little or no desire to work as a team with his owner. A vicious Aussie is not reliable, and that makes him unstable as a companion or working dog. If an Aussie is very nervous or worries a lot, it overrides his ability to work. A very dominant Aussie will always want to do things his way, which can exasperate even the most experienced handler.

By the same token, an Australian Shepherd can have the best temperament in the world, but if he has no herding instinct he will be of little help to the rancher. He may make a great obedience, agility, or companion dog, but he is not likely to find or keep employment as a herding dog.

Coat

An Australian Shepherd's coat is a true working-dog coat. At the risk of sounding redundant, it is important to think about the breed's function as a herding dog in the harsh, wet, and frequently unforgiving climate of the American West. To keep him warm and dry, an Aussie's coat is double-layered—he has a water-resistant outer coat and a shorter, dense, insulating undercoat. Designed to act as a protective layer against water, the undercoat is capable of enduring all weathers, shedding out in the early summer as temperatures begin to rise. It requires regular grooming to prevent matting and to allow a new undercoat to grow in during the late fall or early winter.

Show dogs are frequently favored for their beautiful, full coats, but an Aussie should never be dripping with coat. An excessive amount of coat is inefficient for a herding dog. No farmer or rancher would want that type of coat on his Aussies. With a coat of *medium texture, straight to wavy, weather resistant, of moderate length with an undercoat*, as called for in the standard, there is less chance of debris—such as snow, mud, manure, stickers, burrs, and whatnot—collecting on a dog's belly and legs and between the pads on his feet, any of which can slow down or even impede a dog's movement. Can you imagine an exhausted shepherd sitting around the campfire grooming his Australian Shepherd? Spending countless hours each night picking out cockleburs, sand burs, seedpods, mud, or manure? I think not.

Color

The Australian Shepherd's colors and his unique and amazing array of markings are perhaps the most distinguishing and identifying feature of the breed. The breed comes in four colors: solid black, blue merle, solid red, and red merle; all with or without white markings and/or tan points. The colors must be strong, clear, and rich. People tend to have their favorite colors, but none of the accepted colors are judged

Aussies are intelligent, versatile, and usually easy to train.

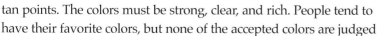

Aussie colors can include (from left to right): black-tri, blue merle, red-tri, and red merle.

or given preference over another as long as the color is within the guidelines of the breed standard. Be wary of anyone trying to sell you a "rare" colored Aussie. The colors listed in the breed standard are the only recognized colors.

An Aussie's basic coat color is either black (jet black) or red. The blacks may be solid black, black with either white trim or copper points (black bi), or black with both white trim and copper points (black tri). Red dogs can range in color and can include deep liver, burgundy, sorrel, mahogany, auburn, shades of rust or chestnut, with or without white markings and/or tan points.

Merling is a modification of the basic black or red color. Blue merle dogs are actually black dogs with parts of the black coat broken up into irregularly shaped patches of gray. The merling is the gray parts of the coat and can be powder blue, silver blue, steel gray, or blue black. Red merles are genetically solid red dogs with parts of their coat broken up into irregular patches of red or liver.

Aussies can be heavily merled, meaning most of their coat is merled with only a patch or two of solid color; lightly merled with coats that are predominantly red or black with just a touch of merling; or anything in between.

Although the AKC, ASCA, and KC standards differ in their terminology, the bottom line is they are all quite explicit when it comes to acceptable colors and white markings—and for good reason, too: The Australian Shepherd is susceptible to serious health problems

associated with the presence of two merling genes. This topic is discussed in greater detail in Chapter eight.

Head, Eyes, and Teeth

Head

Your Aussie's head houses his brain, teeth, ears, eyes, and nose, and is one of the most defining characteristics of breed type. Once you know the breed, it is not difficult to recognize an Aussie head—especially in silhouette. The head described in the ASCA standard is slightly different from that described in the AKC and KC standards. ASCA wants a *flat to slightly rounded* top skull, whereas the AKC and KC standards see a topline of the back skull and muzzle forming parallel planes.

Clean-cut is an important term used to describe an Aussie head that is clearly outlined and free of extra or loose skin, wrinkles, and pendulous lips. The mounds of loose skin on a Bloodhound's head help him to scent and follow a track, but this type of head on an Aussie would be out of place and dangerous. An Aussie with drooping or loose-fitting eyelids would be more susceptible to injury from the accumulation of dirt, dust, twigs, stickers, burrs, and the like. Can you imagine an Aussie with Bloodhound-type lips trying to grip a 1,500-pound range bull or a angry mother cow? His lips would be tattered and torn long before breakfast!

Did You Know?

According to historians, the true blue merle comes from the old name "blue marled" or marbled.

Aussies with lighter-colored eyes do not have any problems seeing.

Eyes

The Aussies' almond-shaped eyes are created not by the eyeball itself, which is always round, but rather by the tissue and bone surrounding the eye. An Aussie's correct head and facial structure allows the eyes to be set obliquely, meaning the outer corners are slightly higher than the inner corners, which forms the almond shape. This configuration affords better protection in a working environment because they are less likely to sustain injury than are the round or protruding eyes of, say, a Chihuahua. The KC standard calls for eyes that are *oval shaped, of moderate size, neither protruding nor sunken.* Many experts feel that sunken or protruding eyes detract from the intelligent and attentive expression of the breed, giving him more of a startled appearance.

Acceptable eye colors are brown, blue, amber, or any variation or combination including flecks and marbling depending on coat color. People unfamiliar with the breed often assume, albeit incorrectly, that Aussies with lighter-colored eyes, especially light blue eyes, have limited vision or are blind. It is not unusual to hear comments, such as "Is your dog blind?" or "Does your dog have a glass eye?" In reality, light-colored eyes simply have less pigmentation than dark-colored eyes.

Teeth

The term *dentition* is a fancy Latin term that refers to the number and arrangement of teeth. Aussie puppies should have 28 teeth (12 incisors, 4 canines, and 12 premolars). Adult Aussies should have a full complement of teeth, meaning 42 adult teeth—22 in the upper jaw (six molars, eight premolars, two canines, and six incisors) and 20 in the upper jaw (four molars, eight premolars, two canines, six incisors).

The ASCA standard calls for a scissors bite because it is considered anatomically correct and the most functional bite, allowing an Aussie to "grip with a pinching bite and eat without wear on the teeth." A scissors bite allows your Aussie to remove burrs and stickers from his coat and foot pads, and allows females to sever a puppy's umbilical cord. The severely undershot jaw of a Bulldog, for example, would be utterly useless on an Aussie because of its vulnerability and unstableness. One can imagine how an undershot jaw might shatter were it to come in contact with the hoof of a willful cow.

Teeth that are missing or broken as a result of an accident are not penalized. Undershot bites and overshot bites exceeding 1/8-inch (3.2 cm) are disqualifications in both ASCA and AKC standards because they severely weaken the overall jaw assembly. While the AKC and KC standards allow a level bite, ASCA faults it because it feels any leniency will "lead to a proliferation of bad bites."

Forequarters, Hindquarters, and Feet

Forequarters

The forequarters, hindquarters, and feet comprise your Aussie's all-important running gear. His forequarters, the combined front assembly that includes the shoulder blade down to the toes and everything in between—humerus, radius, ulna, and feet—support nearly 70 percent of his entire body weight. The forequarters act like shock absorbers to help reduce the jar on a dog's legs when he stops or when he is running on hard surfaces. A good front is essential for efficiency, endurance, speed, dodging horns and hooves, and turning on a dime. A good front assemblage is essential not only for the working Aussie, but also for those competing in agility, obedience, flyball, weight pull, Schutzhund, search and rescue, and so forth.

Hindquarters

The hindquarters comprise the rear assemblage and include everything from the pelvis down to the toes. A correct hindquarter assemblage provides a dog with maximum drive (extension of the rear legs), lift, and power for propulsion. The correct angulation between the pelvis and the femur (thigh bone) gives your Aussie adequate bend in his stifles (knees) and allows for speed and endurance.

The Australian Shepherd's forequarters and hindquarters must be proportionate and compatible for him to function efficiently as a whole. If a dog's front or rear assembly is out of sync, it produces a variety of gaiting problems that can include crabbing, overreaching, pacing, not converging on the center of gravity, and so forth. A poorly assembled forequarter or hindquarter interferes with a dog's speed

Eye Problems

Aussies are susceptible to a variety of eye problems, which are discussed in detail in Chapter eight.

25

The Aussie's forequarters and hindquarters are built for speed and endurance.

and power, cutting down on his efficiency and ability to do his job with the greatest amount of ease.

Feet

As a herding dog, Aussies are often required to cover long distances over varying terrains and in all weather. Strong, sound feet and thick pads are essential. Stickers, burrs, stubble, and sharp stones would wreck havoc with thin pads in a very short time.

The AKC, ASCA, and KC standards call for feet that are oval, compact with well-arched toes, and thick pads. A compact foot gives an Australian Shepherd the greatest amount of strength and spring, allowing for maximum endurance and agility.

Gait

Gait describes a dog's movement, such as a walk, canter, trot, or gallop. Efficiency and endurance are paramount for a working Aussie. He needs stamina to travel great distances and keep going for hours on end. He needs exceptional athletic ability—to run as fast as the wind, switch directions instantly, and spring into immediate action if a sheep or cow decides to get out of line. Any wasted movement expends valuable energy and contributes to early fatigue—a disastrous situation for working Aussies.

To maximize both efficiency and endurance, an Aussie utilizes several gaits but depends primarily on a trot. Considered the most energy-efficient gait for sustained travel, the trot should be smooth, fluid, and efficient with little or no side-to-side or up-and-down movement. When necessary, Aussies also utilize a gallop to accelerate, as when outrunning a wayward ewe, a willful cow, or kids fleeing on bicycles.

In the show ring, the Aussie's physical structure is evaluated at a trot of moderate speed because his structural strengths and weaknesses are more clearly visible at a trot. A dog is moved on a loose leash while "coming and going"—going away from and coming back to the judge in a straight line, and also while trotting side-on to the judge.

Size, Proportion, and Substance

Size

Your Aussie's ancestors were originally bred to control sheep and cattle that frequently outweighed them by more than 1,000 pounds. The forefathers of the breed needed a dog who was sturdy, fast, and agile—not too *coarse* (large and clunky) or too *weedy* (small and fragile.) The AKC standard describes the Aussie as *solidly built with moderate bone. Structure in the male reflects masculinity without coarseness. Bitches appear feminine without being slight of bone.*

Size is also an important factor in establishing breed type. One does not, for example, think of Australian Shepherds as being the size of the low-set Welsh Corgis or the taller Belgian Tervurens. Although AKC, ASCA, and KC standards state that the height at the withers varies from 20 to 23 inches (51 to 58 cms) for males, and from 18 to 21 inches (46 to 52 cms) for females, working Aussie owners never favor a particular height over herding ability and, indeed, the AKC and ASCA standards note *quality is not to be sacrificed in favor of size.*

In his book, *Sweet Promised Land,* Robert Laxalt recounts how his father, Dominique Laxalt, a shepherd in Nevada during the early 1900s, wrapped his dogs' feet in burlap to keep them from bleeding. While the dogs were tough "with strong legs and feet like leather" — the rocky hillsides were unforgiving, and "even a man's boots wouldn't last two weeks."

Proportion

The key component when discussing any aspect of the Australian Shepherd is proportion. Some call it *balance* or *harmonious balance* or even *symmetry*. Regardless of the terminology, the Australian Shepherd must be correctly proportioned, well balanced and, according to the standards, *slightly longer than tall, of medium size and bone…he is lithe and agile, solid and muscular without cloddiness.* His length of body helps to give him his ground-covering stride, and is considered the best body type for sustained trotting and endurance.

With the acceptance of the Australian Shepherd by the AKC, it is

The key to a proper Aussie look is balance.

not unusual to see differences in the physical size and appearance between working Aussies and Aussies bred for the show ring. Generally speaking, working Aussies also tend to be slimmer and fitter than their show-ring counterparts. Australian Shepherds who are too heavy lose their maneuverability, agility, and endurance. An overweight Aussie is also at risk for developing a variety of health problems, which are discussed in subsequent chapters.

Aussie Tails

A hallmark of the Aussie breed is his docked (surgically removed) or bobbed tail. ASCA and AKC breed standards clearly state that an Australian Shepherd's tail is docked or naturally bobbed. The Kennel Club allows for the exhibition of docked, naturally bobbed, or undocked tails. In England, the docking of tails is legal if carried out by a veterinary surgeon. In Germany and other countries, the practice is forbidden, and Aussies are exhibited with tails.

Herding Instinct

Years ago, Aussies were selectively bred and developed specifically for their working abilities. Today, herding instinct remains a fundamental characteristic of the working stock dog. Like any inherited characteristic, some Aussies have a lot, some have a little, and others have zero herding instinct. Aussies bred from strong working/herding stock have a better chance of inheriting the necessary characteristics than those Aussies bred from strong show/conformation lines. Good working Aussies must have, to some degree, trainability, eye (see below), and power. Ideally, Aussies should have a good balance of these characteristics. However, what owners want and what they get are seldom one and the same.

Eye

Eye is a fascinating characteristic of herding dogs in general. Difficult to define but easy to recognize once you understand it, some describe *eye* as a style of concentration, or an "intense gaze" that gives an Aussie the power to control and move livestock. In his book, *The Farmer's Dog*, author John Holmes writes, "It is really far more an attitude of approach than anything connected with the dog's eye."

Eye is an inherited characteristic, and many experts think it evolved in wolves to help them stalk their prey. Man supposedly developed that eye into something more useful, particularly in the Border Collie, who uses his eye in combination with a stalking style of movement to control, hold, or pressure stock into moving. Most Aussies don't stare as intently and continually as their Border Collie counterparts. Aussies look around more, and they rely more on body movement to exert or relieve pressure and get the stock moving.

Aussies, as well as all herding dogs, need a certain amount of eye to be effective working dogs. Otherwise, they have no real connection to the livestock. By the same token, too much eye creates a "sticky" dog—a dog with too much hesitation in his approach. A sticky dog lacks power because he tends to fixate his gaze on one particular sheep, often the first one he comes to. A sticky dog can be nose-to-nose with a stubborn ewe and be unable to move her.

The type of livestock being worked make a difference in how much eye a person wants in a dog. Handlers usually like a dog who has a medium eye but, as with nearly everything pertaining to Aussies, it's a matter of preference.

Herding dogs also need *power*, and that power must be in balance

A Tale of Tails

Perhaps nothing is more controversial in the Aussie breed standard than the practice of tail docking. The practice, while not indigenous to the Australian Shepherd breed, is a tradition that has come under fire for many years. Some theorize the practice dates to the early Romans—who believed it prevented rabies. Debated in the late 1700s, there is also the theory of acquired characteristics. Put simply, if the mother and father dogs had no tails—the puppies would acquire the no-tail look of their parents. Perhaps the most common accumulated traditions and beliefs are those associated with working, herding, and hunting dogs. Docking the tails of livestock dogs was a common practice among herdsmen 150 years ago, and legend has it that these dogs were exempt from a luxury tax that was imposed on owners of nonworking dogs. As a result, owners of working dogs docked their dogs' tails as a way to document the dogs' lawful and tax-free occupation. These dogs frequently worked in varying environmental conditions, and it is believed a dog's tail was docked to reduce his susceptibility to injury from dense vegetation, briars, sticks, burrs, and the like.

Herdsman also believed a dog's tail acted as a rudder, and they supposedly docked the tail as a way to reduce maneuverability, which, allegedly, discouraged a dog's fondness and inclination for chasing an assortment of critters including jackrabbits and deer.

Finally, there is the theory that tails were docked for hygienic reasons including preventing feces from collecting around the base of the tail, which, in addition to being generally unpleasant, could lead to bacteria accumulation, flies, and maggots.

We may never know for certain the true reason, but we do know that Aussies were sporting the no-tail look long before ASCA or AKC developed a breed standard, and it remains a clearly identifiable characteristic of the breed.

A herding dog's "eye" is often described as an "intense gaze" used to control and move livestock.

with the dog's eye. Power is not about the physical strength, size, or structure of an Aussie. Think of it as more of an intimidation factor—whether or not sheep fear the dog. Sheep have a natural fear of dogs and the uncanny ability to know exactly which dogs to fear; which dogs will stand up to them, chase them, or bite them; which dogs have the power to make them move; and which dogs do not.

Dogs with a lot of power are often said to be *hard*—meaning a dog that is very keen, may be difficult to slow up or control, but has the power to move a stubborn ewe across a creek or stream. A hard dog thinks he knows more about livestock than does his owner—and usually he does! This type of dog can try the patience of even the most experienced and knowledgeable dog handler. At the other end of the spectrum are *soft* dogs—dogs with little or no power to move any ewe, let alone a stubborn one. In between the extremes of hard and soft dogs are the moderate dogs. Softer than the hardest dogs, but not so soft that they do not have any power, they are middle-of-the-road dogs, so to speak.

A dog with the proper balance of eye and power can move stock where it may not necessarily want to go. If needed, he will show a stubborn ewe or rank bull who is boss. "You will move or I will make you move." This type of dog can also stand his ground in the face of intimidation, with a gaze that clearly says, "Don't even think about it!"

CHARACTERISTICS OF THE AUSTRALIAN SHEPHERD

Theoretically, the breed standard describes the ideal temperament of the Australian Shepherd. In the real world, Aussies run the gamut in temperaments, and the genetic lottery can produce Aussies who are happy-go-lucky, mellow, shy, sulky, sassy, fearful, or dog-to-dog aggressive. Some Aussies are whizzes at working livestock, but fearful of humans. Others dislike children. Some are noise- or sight-sensitive. Some hold a grudge, while others are dominant and pushy. Most are high-octane dogs who love to be included in every activity, be it biking, swimming, or riding shotgun in the family car.

The best indicator of a puppy's temperament is the disposition of his mother and father. That said, human ignorance, environmental influences, and conditions under which a puppy is whelped, reared, and socialized also play an important part in defining his temperament.

When acquired from a reputable breeder, Aussie pups usually possess the classic Aussie temperament and are happy, funny, devoted, and seldom take life too seriously. As a general rule, viciousness is not a problem in Aussies. In those rare instances, owner ignorance, bad handling, or a hereditary defect are primary causes.

Most knowledgeable breeders can match the personality and temperament of a particular dog with the right family, which makes acquiring an Aussie from a reputable breeder doubly important.

Personality Profile

Most Aussies—especially those coming from the strong working lines—have type-A personalities, with get-it-done-right-now attitudes. They have a century-old heritage as working dogs, and they are not happy sitting around the house all day or pacing back and forth in a kennel. Working Aussies are bred for courage, longevity, and staying

Most Aussies are type-A personalities, with "get it done now" attitudes.

power. The working stiffs of the herding world, they can move a thousand head of sheep across a thousand acres; push cattle up steep mountain slopes; handle the rankest bull or maddest mother cow; go to the nose of a stubborn ewe; and, on rare occasions, move incredibly large wild bison for the Department of Interior. They have tireless endurance, often working all day with only an occasionally rest break.

The qualities that make them exceptional working dogs are the very qualities that can make them unsuitable as suburban pets. In the absence of adequate physical and mental stimulation, Aussies can quickly become bored and destructive.

A by-product of their herding instinct is their penchant for attacking moving objects including lawnmowers, weed-whackers, and vacuum cleaners. Rakes, brooms, and snow shovels are equally stimulating to them. More than a few have been surrendered to humane societies, abandoned, or given to rescue organizations because of their propensity to tear after rambunctious children—biting and nipping at their ankles.

The Key to Success

Matching the right dog with the right owner is the key to a happy and successful human–canine relationship. It's a fact that not all Aussies make good pets. Few, if any, working Aussies detox from their natural instincts. Some Aussies are too active and intense for the average dog owner. They can be pushy and bossy, and they always think they are smarter than their owner (and many times they are!). These dogs can make good pets, but it takes an experienced dog person to manage and bring out the best in them. To put them in the hands of an inexperienced dog person or to relegate them to the isolation of a backyard is nothing short of cruelty.

Equally important, there is no such thing as a part-time Aussie. You must educate yourself about the breed and understand the time and energy requirements necessary to live harmoniously with an intelligent, high-drive, high-energy dog. You must commit yourself to establishing a human–canine relationship that is built on a mutual foundation of love, respect, and trust; start obedience lessons right away; continue to reinforce the commands throughout his entire life; and understand that first and foremost the Australian Shepherd is a working dog who needs a job. Couch potatoes, workaholics, or full-time moms with a new baby might want to seriously consider, say, a Bulldog, who is known for his

Miniature Australian Shepherds

Miniature and toy Australian Shepherds are becoming increasing popular as pets. However, they are not recognized by the American Kennel Club, the United States Australian Shepherd Association, or the Australian Shepherd Club of America. Both ASCA and USASA strongly oppose the purposeful breeding of miniature Aussies, and do not recognize these dogs as Australian Shepherds.

Your Aussie should live with you, as a member of the family.

low-energy lifestyle.

Most important, you need a sense of humor and a great deal of strength and commitment if things begin to go wrong. Once you've mastered all that—owning an Australian Shepherd is nothing more than a full-time job.

LIVING WITH AN AUSTRALIAN SHEPHERD

What do these intelligent, high-energy dogs need to be happy and healthy companions?

Living Arrangements

In an ideal world, all Aussies would live on farms and ranches with an array of chores to keep them physically and mentally stimulated. Many Aussies do live in working or rural environments, but a large portion also live in suburbia and big cities. Generally speaking, Aussies do not make great apartment dogs—unless, of course, you can devote time to multiple and extended exercise excursions, say five or six times a day. Their working instinct, high energy levels, and physical and mental requirements can turn apartment living into a nightmare for both dog and owner—and landlord! That said, some Aussies are naturally calmer and less energetic than others, and you may be able to find one who is more suited to apartment or townhouse living. An older Aussie, for instance, may be more suited to your lifestyle. Overall, however, 99.9 percent of Aussies do not adapt well to a sedentary lifestyle.

No matter where you live, your Aussie should live with you, *not* relegated to the isolation of a backyard or tethered on a chain. This is neither fair nor humane. Aussies are not a breed that does well unattended—they need social interaction with their owners. Despite their size and abundance of energy, Aussies can and do make excellent house dogs when they receive appropriate training and exercise.

A securely fenced yard or kennel area is an absolute must for those times when your Aussie must be outside to relieve himself or be left alone for short periods. The fence must be at least 6 feet tall and equipped with secure latches or locks that intruders, curious children, or talented and determined Aussies cannot open.

Regardless of whether you live in the city, suburbia, or the country, never allow your Aussie to roam at will. Unsupervised dogs can wreak havoc on livestock, not to mention your neighbors' cherished vegetable or flower garden. Free-roaming Aussies can be stolen, hit by a car, poisoned, or shot by neighboring farmers or ranchers. They can be injured or killed fighting with other animals, or lost forever.

Exercise Needs

Dogs need plenty of exercise to maintain their good health, just like humans. Exercise is vital for stimulating your Australian Shepherd's circulatory system, building strong bones and muscles, and nourishing and energizing his mind, which keeps him active, healthy, and alert. Exercise wards off obesity—keeping your Aussie fit and lean. Exercise and interactive play eliminates loneliness, stress, and boredom, which are often the primary causes of problem behaviors including destructive chewing and chronic barking. You'll also be giving your

A healthy adult Aussie will require more than a walk around the block to satisfy his exercise requirements.

Aussie plenty of attention while building a strong human–canine relationship. Contrary to popular opinion, most dogs will not exercise themselves in the backyard—regardless of how big their fenced yard might be. Most Aussies will sit at the door—or chew, dig, and bark to amuse themselves—while they wait for their owners to come outside and play with them.

You must tailor an exercise program to suit your Australian Shepherd—taking into account his age, health, and overall physical condition. A puppy, for example, will tire more quickly than an adult dog. Therefore, a puppy will require short but multiple exercise periods spaced throughout the day. You also must be careful with your Aussie puppy. He may act tough, but his little body can easily be injured when jumping, twisting, turning, or getting body slammed by a bigger dog. A healthy adult Aussie, on the other hand, will require more than a brisk walk around the block to satisfy his energy needs. Most Aussies can work from sunup to sundown and still

Exercise Your Senior

It's important not to neglect the exercise needs of your older Aussie. A senior dog needs exercise to keep his body functioning properly. The exercise will not be as strenuous as a younger dog's, but should be regular and enough to keep him active, alert, and healthy.

have energy to herd the kids or play a game of fetch. Again, much will depend on your dog's overall physical and mental health and individual energy level.

Mental exercise is just as important as physical exercise. Try to come up with fun games that stimulate your Aussie's brain. For example, teach him tricks like wave, walk backwards, spin, twist, speak, jump through a hoop, find a ball hidden in a box or under a bucket, or retrieve his food bowl when he's done eating.

As with any exercise program, it is important to start slow and gradually work your way up to higher levels. Your Aussie is susceptible to heat stroke. Therefore, it is best to confine your exercise and training to the cooler parts of the day. If you notice signs of fatigue, including heavy panting, allow your Aussie plenty of time to rest and cool down. If your Aussie is overweight, injured, or out of condition, consult your veterinarian before beginning any exercise program.

Australian Shepherds and Other Pets

Australian Shepherds are quintessential ranch and farm dogs, and most ranches have an abundance of different animals, including other dogs, horses, goats, cats, chickens, and llamas. With proper socialization and a good dose of common sense, you can teach your Aussie to live happily and harmoniously with other animals.

It is important to introduce your Aussie to other animals in a safe, positive, and controlled environment—one in which you are controlling the situation, not the dog! The bottom line is management and expectations. What type of behaviors will you accept? Hopefully, you won't tolerate chasing, harassing, or bullying the cat, the horse, or other dogs! Manage the situation so that your Aussie is not allowed to develop bad or fearful behaviors.

Make sure your puppy has positive experiences with other dogs. If other dogs bully your puppy, he could grow into an adult dog who is fearful of other dogs. Dogs run, chase, play bite, tug at body parts, yip, yap, body slam, and knock each other down. Most of the time, it is great fun for the dogs—provided both dogs are enjoying the game. How do you tell when a fun game has crossed over into a brawl? Watch both dogs' body language—the dog chasing and the dog being chased. Are your Aussie's ears up? Is he returning the play or trying to get away? Is your dog nervous or frightened? Is he cowering, or is his tail between his legs? Is your Aussie too big for the other dogs?

Young dogs or very small dogs can inadvertently be injured when tussling with bigger, more powerful puppies. In any of these situations, it is always best to err on the side of caution.

Australian Shepherds and Children

If you navigated adolescence with an Aussie, or any dog for that matter, you were surely loved. You passed the days playing together. He probably tracked mud in the house, licked your face, shared your lunch, nipped at your pant legs and, at the end of the day collapsed on your bed in a heap of sleep. In retrospect, one might question how either of you (or your parents) survived the chaos and craziness—not to mention the germs! Aussies can be the most delightful of childhood companions, but they require guidance.

A good-natured Aussie can live quite well with children who understand how to respect the family pet.

Living harmoniously with kids and Aussies in today's society is possible. First and foremost, it is important to understand that dogs are pack animals. They have a clearly defined chain of command. They respect members of the pack who are higher up in rank than they are, and they have no respect for members of the pack who are lower. It's that simple.

The leader of your "pack" must always be you. Otherwise, dogs, like toddlers and teenagers, quickly learn which family members are easily manipulated. As the pack leader and a responsible dog owner, it is up to you to teach your puppy—and your children—which behaviors are acceptable and which are not. This takes time and effort on your part, but it allows your puppy to grow into a well-behaved adult dog capable of living in the human world.

Most good-natured Australian Shepherds do quite well in a household when they are raised with children, established guidelines are followed, and children are clearly supervised. Aussies may be tough enough to move a stubborn ewe across a creek bed or send 1,000 sheep into a dipping tank, but even the most accepting Aussie may not tolerate the rough-and-tumble behavior of young kids who try to smother them with affection, tug on their ears or tails, bang pots on their heads, or poke little fingers in their eyes. These types of behaviors can startle, frighten, and even injure an Australian Shepherd.

Teaching Children about Dogs

Parents are key figures when it comes to teaching children how to interact safely with a dog, including how to pet him, feed him, hug him, talk to him, and play with him. From day one, it is important that you teach your child some basic common courtesies that apply to equally to the family dog as they do to other family members. For example, you would not allow a child to jump on a parent or sibling who is sleeping, or barge into a bathroom without knocking. The same considerations apply to the family dog, such as teaching children not to disturb a dog who is sleeping, eating, or chewing a bone.

Many children under the age of 7 do not understand the consequences of their actions. They see nothing wrong with trying to pick up a puppy by his ears or clutching him for dear life. They do not understand they can seriously injure a puppy or young dog if they pick him up incorrectly or drop him. Your Aussie may respond by fleeing the area, growling, or biting. It's his way of saying, "Leave me alone, I'm eating" or "Pull my ear one more time, and you'll be sorry!"

At the other end of the spectrum, when a puppy is allowed to play unsupervised with several young children, you end up with an adult dog who has learned to chase, jump, and nip at arms and legs in motion. Motion stimulates an Aussie's natural instinct to chase and nip. Left unchecked, your puppy will see no harm in continuing this "game" when he is a 50-pound (23-kg) adult dog.

Aussies are attracted to noise. Remember the weed-whacker and vacuum? Children who run and scream while playing are as good as

Does Gender Make a Difference?

Generally speaking, dogs of the opposite sex are less likely to squabble or fight. Long before dogs were domesticated, they lived in packs, and survival was based on a hierarchal system. Males fought other males mainly to establish their position in the group. Rather than fight to the death, the loser survived because that was in the best interest of maintaining the species. Even today, fighting males will growl, snap, bite, make a lot of noise, wreak a lot of havoc, and cause a lot of damage until a human intervenes or the subordinate dog cries "Uncle." On the other hand, a female's aggression stems from the instinct to protect her babies. Survival of the enemy was of no particular interest to her. For this reason, fights between females generally have more severe consequences than encounters between males.

If well-socialized, your Aussie can get along with other pets.

sheep to an Australian Shepherd. It is the Aussies' nature to control his flock—to prevent them from escaping, and to bring back to the group any sheep that have strayed. The behavior of nipping and biting at the children's ankles is not an aggressive act, but rather an instinctual behavior that has been genetically programmed for hundreds of years. In the dog's eyes, your children (his flock) are getting away, and he is simply trying to control them. It is important that you understand and recognize this type of behavior so you can nip it in the bud immediately.

Equally important, infants, babies, and young children should never, ever, ever under any circumstances be left alone with a dog regardless of how trustworthy your Aussie may be. No dog is completely predictable with children. A dog may misread the strange sounds of an infant or the unpredictable behaviors of a toddler.

Children who learn how to properly care for their dog learn responsibility, respect, and compassion. They learn that he needs water when he is thirsty, food when he is hungry, a bath when he is dirty, and peace and quiet when he is sleeping. At what age you begin teaching these responsibilities varies depending on the individual child. There are some things you can teach a 4-year-old child, but not a 3-year-old. A child's individual maturity level dictates how much responsibility to give him in any part of life, including the responsibility of feeding and caring for a dog.

The Finer Points of Play

Play is a wonderful releaser of excess energy for both dogs and kids, but kids also must be taught what games are acceptable when playing with dogs. To prevent the situation from getting out of control, parents should always monitor and control the play between dogs and kids; play should be appropriate to the size and age of the dog as well as the child. Think *active* rather than rough—avoid games that encourage or allow a dog to use his teeth, such as sic 'em, or attack or wrestling games, where a dog can become overexcited and inadvertently learn to use his teeth. Children should never be allowed to hit, kick, pinch, punch, bite, or harass your Aussie—or any dog—in the name of play.

PREPARING

for Your Australian Shepherd

Australian Shepherds are intelligent, high-drive, high-energy dogs, and deciding to add one to your family is not a decision to be taken lightly—especially when you consider that a well-bred, well-cared for Aussie can live upwards of 15 years. The Aussie's loyalty, devotion, and strong desire to please help to make him one of America's most endearing breeds; however, his non-stop energy, strong working instincts, and uncanny ability to get into all sorts of trouble can make him a poor choice for novice or first-time dog owners.

Caring for any breed of dog is a lot of hard work because a dog cannot take care of himself. For his entire lifetime, your Aussie will depend on you for his food, water, shelter, exercise, grooming, training, love, hugs, kisses, and regular veterinary care. He will look to you for companionship at all hours of the day. He will want to play when you want to relax. He will try to herd the kids, the cats, other dogs, horses, and even the vacuum cleaner. It's highly likely he will occasionally track mud through the house, refuse to come when he's called, and embarrass you in front of your friends, neighbors, and in-laws. The good news is he will also make you laugh harder than you ever thought possible.

PUPPY OR ADULT?

If you are convinced that an Australian Shepherd is the right breed for you, you still have some decisions to make. The first one is: Do you want a puppy or an adult dog?

Puppies

If you decide to acquire a puppy, as opposed to an older dog, you'll be starting with a clean slate. The puppy has no bad habits (yet!), and you can maximize his potential by shaping his character, fostering his fun personality, and instilling all the behaviors he will need to function as he grows bigger and bolder. You set your own expectations and manage your puppy so that he grows into a well-rounded, well-behaved adult dog.

On the other hand, raising a puppy is a lot of work. Why do you think puppies are cute and adorable? If they weren't, who in their right mind would spend 24 hours a day at their beck and call—feeding, pottying, and cleaning up after them? Unfortunately, that is why a lot of Aussies end up in humane societies: When the cuteness wears off, they still need to be trained, groomed, fed, exercised, and loved on a daily basis.

Raising a puppy is similar to raising a human baby. Both are demanding and require enormous amounts of time and energy—at all hours of the day and usually in the middle of the night. Puppies left to their own devices get into all kinds of mischief—barking, chewing, digging, and peeing on the rug. A puppy must be housetrained and obedience trained. He needs guidance and direction, so that he doesn't bark all night, chase other animals, or dig holes in your newly planted vegetable garden.

An Aussie puppy requires a great deal of socialization. It's absolutely essential if you want to raise a well-behaved, nonaggressive adult Aussie. Invest time taking him to puppy kindergarten, walks in the park, and rides in the car. Expose him to every possible situation he is likely to encounter as an adult, such as people riding bicycles, kids on skateboards, joggers, men in baseball hats, other animals, trash cans, sprinklers, and people in wheelchairs. Raising a puppy is a rewarding and life-changing experience, but a lot of work! Don't let anyone tell you otherwise.

Adult Dogs

No one can deny that puppies are cute, but there's a lot to be said for a well-trained adult dog. When you acquire an older Australian Shepherd (often 1, 2, or 3 years old), what you see is what you get. An older dog's personality is already developed, and his herding instinct, drive, and energy level are well established. With close observation, interaction, and help from a knowledgeable dog person, you should be able to determine the quality of his disposition and whether he will suit your personality and daily life. Is he timid? Aggressive? Nervous? Does he have ants in his pants? Is he energetic? Happy? Is he spoiled rotten? Does he get along with other animals? How is he around children?

Adult Aussies become available for a variety of reasons. Many breeders have one- or two-year-old herding, obedience, agility, or show prospects who did not pan out for a variety of reasons, but would make exceptional pets in the right home. Occasionally, adult dogs are returned to the breeder because the owner moved or is no longer able to keep the dog. Many of these dogs are well bred and have been well cared for, yet, for one reason or another, need to be placed in a good home.

If you see an Aussie advertised "Free to Good Home" in local papers, you can assume it's code for "The dog has bad habits, he's driving me crazy, and I don't want him anymore." These dogs are often lacking in direction, management, and love, and have been allowed to develop annoying habits. In the right hands, they can make wonderful pets—but go in with your eyes wide open.

Purchasing an adult dog is not without risk, either. A retired show dog will most likely be socialized, crate-trained, and accustomed to traveling, but he may not be housetrained. An Aussie from strong working lines may be too energetic or intense. Some adult dogs have been allowed to develop quirks, bad behaviors, or obsessive-compulsive behaviors that are difficult if not impossible for the inexperienced owner to manage. Some Aussies have not been raised around kids, and they may not like kids. Some children are more active and vocal than others, and this can annoy even the most stable dog. Most reputable breeders will want to meet your children and observe how they behave and interact around dogs, and vice versa. Absent any problems, most kids and Australian Shepherds who are properly introduced and supervised can develop a strong and loving relationship that lasts a lifetime.

MALE OR FEMALE?

Choosing a male or female dog usually comes down to personal preference. Some people are attracted to the strength and masculinity of a male dog. Others love the femininity and slight refinement of a female. Generally speaking, females tend to mature physically a bit earlier than do males. As a result, females might be more serious or emotionally more mature at a younger age. However, both males and females can make sweet, loving companions, and there are pros and cons

You'll have to decide if you want a puppy or an adult.

Most kids and Australian Shepherds who are properly introduced and supervised can develop a strong and loving relationship that lasts a lifetime.

to both sexes. If you already own a dog—regardless of the breed—and are thinking of adding an Aussie, consider a dog of the opposite sex who is (or will be) spayed or neutered. If, for example, you already own a male dog, consider getting a female and vice versa. Dogs of the opposite sex are less likely to create chaos and turmoil in terms of fighting and squabbling, and some females—despite your best intentions—simply will not live together happily.

When it comes to choosing an Aussie, knowledgeable breeders know the capabilities of both sexes and are your best bet when choosing a dog who suits your temperament, personality, and lifestyle.

FINDING THE AUSTRALIAN SHEPHERD WHO'S RIGHT FOR YOU

Australian Shepherds are a true red, white, and blue success story, but they are not a breed for everyone. Finding one that suits your personality and lifestyle requires time and a bit of detective work. Do your homework and check on resources, familiarize yourself with the Aussie breed standard, and research the best places to find your dog. Sadly, some people breed Australian Shepherds purely for money, with little interest in the future welfare of the dog. Talk to trainers, veterinarians, and other Aussie owners. Separate opinion from fact, which can be a daunting task for the newcomer.

Experience Counts

Breeding purebred dogs is a labor of love, as well as an art and a science. Experienced Aussie people are usually conscientious, dog-smart, and care about the welfare of their dogs and the breed. They study pedigrees, plan litters, and breed only to maintain or improve the quality of the Aussie breed. Great care and forethought is put into their breeding program. Breeding stock is tested for genetic problems including hip dysplasia and cataracts, and only those dogs who are proven clear of problems are used for breeding. Puppies are regularly and affectionately socialized to everything they are likely to encounter as adult dogs. Puppies are evaluated to assess training requirements, competitive potential, and placement options.

Experienced Aussie people can answer questions regarding the training, grooming, feeding, and handling of Aussies, and dogs in general. Potential owners are screened, and dogs are sold only to those who meet the qualifications necessary to provide a permanent, first-class home.

Purchasing an Aussie from someone who understands and cares about the breed goes well beyond the sales transaction, because that person will be there to help you through the transition periods, offer training advice, and help you make serious decisions regarding the care and well-being of your Australian Shepherd. If for some reason your particular Aussie does not work out, they are often in a position to either take back the dog, help place it, or offer an appropriate solution.

Backyard Breeders

In your search, it is likely you will come across people who are not interested in the betterment of Australian Shepherds—people who breed dogs with little regard or concern for their dogs' ancestral background, working ability, or the finer points of the Australian Shepherd breed. They are not necessarily bad people, and they do not always have bad intentions. Some of them truly love their dogs and provide good care. However, most are unaware they are contributing to an even larger problem—pet overpopulation.

These "backyard breeders" seldom have knowledge of pedigrees, genetic disorders, or the importance of socializing puppies. Normally, they are not involved in the sport of dogs, nor do they invest the time, money, or energy into producing dogs of sound health and temperament. Their breeding stock is generally not breed quality, meaning it does not meet or exceed the requirements necessary for producing healthy, sound, intelligent, working dogs. Puppies are generally sold on a first-come, first-served basis with little regard for the future welfare or living conditions of the dogs. The dogs are seldom socialized properly, and a backyard breeder is likely to be of no future help to a puppy buyer if things begin to go wrong. They usually wash their hands of the dog before the ink is dry on the check.

Purchasing an Aussie from this type of breeder is a gamble. You may pay less up front for a dog, but it is highly likely that you will pay

Meet the Puppy

Australian Shepherds are fairly popular, but finding the Aussie who is right for you will take some time and plenty of investigating. Puppies can be purchased and shipped long distance, be it across the state or across the country. However, unless you personally know the person, or the kennel has outstanding references, it is always a good idea to meet the puppy first. This allows you to view the facility and see all the dogs. Selling dogs online has become increasingly popular. Unfortunately, not all people who breed dogs are reputable, and the Aussie you purchase online may be a far cry from what arrives at your doorstep.

When speaking to Aussie people and breeders, keep in mind that most are biased in their opinions. Of course they will tell you their puppies are the best! Therefore, it is best to talk to as many people as possible before making your choice.

a good deal more in vet bills—especially if the dog has serious health or temperament problems.

Where to Begin

Breed clubs and registries, such as the Australian Shepherd Club of America (ASCA), United States Australian Shepherd Association (USASA), the American Kennel Club (AKC), and the Kennel Club in the United Kingdom (KC), are good places to start. They can refer you to experts, provide information on the history of the breed, characteristics, and so forth.

Veterinarians are usually familiar with Aussie people, the health of their dogs, and the level of care they provide to their dogs. They can usually provide you with a list of local people who are involved in the sport of dogs in general, and Aussies in particular.

Herding trials and dog shows are an absolute must-do when searching for an Australian Shepherd. They are great fact-finding missions, because the best indicator of a puppy's temperament is his sire and dam. You can compare the quality of many Aussies under one roof, talk to owners and handlers, see how they interact with their dogs, and watch dogs compete in different venues including herding, obedience, agility, and conformation. You can find information about dog shows from Infodog.com, local clubs, or national registries.

Questions to Ask

Educating yourself about the Australian Shepherd's temperament, genetic diseases, exercise requirements, and so forth, will allow you to ask informed questions of the source. Experienced dog people are a valuable source of information, but separating them from the novice or irresponsible breeder can be a challenge if you don't know what you need to know. At the minimum, you will want to know:

- How long have they been involved with Australian Shepherds? (Look for someone who has longevity in the breed.)
- Do they belong to any local or national clubs or organizations?
- Do they compete in canine sports, such as herding, agility, tracking, or obedience?
- Are the dogs registered? (This alone does not guarantee quality.)
- Will they supply a pedigree (three-generation) and/or health certificate?
- Are they willing to take the dog back if things do not work out?
- What is their refund policy?

- Can you contact them if problems arise?
- Have the puppies' eyes been examined by a canine ophthalmologist?
- Have the puppies been dewormed and vaccinated?
- Have the sire and dam been tested for genetic problems (i.e., hip dysplasia, cataracts)?
- Will they supply you with copies of the documentation for the medical and genetic tests?
- How many litters do they breed yearly? (Most responsible dog people produce one, two, or three litters a year. Anything more may indicate a problem.)

What You Will Be Asked

Most people involved in purebred dogs go to great lengths to place their dogs in the best possible homes. They will want to know about you, your family, and the environment in which the Australian Shepherd will be reared. This information helps them to match the right dog with the right owners. For example, a quiet, single adult will need a puppy with a different personality than a family with three or four active kids who like to play sports, hike, and ride bikes. Therefore, you should be prepared—and not offended—when you

Educate yourself about the breed before you begin looking.

It's never a good idea to choose a puppy based entirely on looks. The most adorable Aussie puppy in the litter may not be the best puppy for you. He may be too obsessive, too intense, too energetic. He may be too dominant, too spunky, too sassy, too cheeky. An experienced Aussie person will be able to match the right puppy with your personality and the needs of your family.

encounter a breeder who grills you for information. Some of the many questions she is likely to ask include:

- Why do you want an Australian Shepherd?
- What is your knowledge of the Australian Shepherd breed—and dogs in general?
- Are you familiar with the intelligence and energy level of Aussies?
- Have you ever trained a dog before? What breed?
- Do you currently own an Aussie or any other breed of dog?
- Do you own any other animals, including cats, horses, rabbits, goats?
- What happened to your previous dog? Did he happily grow old? Was he released to a shelter? Did he escape your yard, never to be seen again?
- Will this dog be an indoor or outdoor dog? Or a combination of the two?
- Do you have children? How many—and their ages?
- Are you active and energetic? Are you a workaholic who's never home?
- Do you live in a house? Apartment? The city? Country? Do you rent or own a home?
- Is your yard fenced?

Rescue Organizations

Rescuing a purebred Aussie is a viable option for many prospective owners. Australian Shepherd rescue volunteers work tirelessly to educate the public, as well as to rehabilitate and place purebred Aussies in loving, permanent homes.

Many wonderful, sensitive, and loving Australian Shepherds are surrendered to rescue organizations because their owners did not understand the work and effort required in owning, training, and living with a herding dog. A significant number of owners did not understand nor were they prepared to deal with the behavior problems that result when intelligent, high-energy dogs do not have acceptable physical and mental outlets for their energy. These problems can include chewing, digging, chronic barking, or aggression toward other dogs.

Many Aussies are given up or abandoned after they outgrow the cute stage. Some Aussies in rescue have been abused or mishandled. Many lack proper socialization skills. Others have been accidentally lost or voluntarily relinquished to animal shelters or rescue groups by their owner or their owners' family because of personal illness, death,

or other changes in circumstances. Pregnant bitches or young puppies occasionally find their way into rescue, but the majority of Aussies are older dogs, over 1 year of age.

Rescues carefully evaluate the Aussies in their care via temperament testing. They then place the Aussies in experienced foster homes where they receive veterinary attention, obedience training, socialization, grooming, and lots of love until they can be placed in a permanent home. Countless stories have been told of Australian Shepherds once labelled "difficult" or "untrainable" who went on to excel in canine events, such as obedience, flyball, herding, and agility—proving that dogs can flourish in the hands of responsible owners who know and understand Australian Shepherds.

ILP

Purebred Aussies who are adopted from rescue organizations are eligible to apply for an Indefinite Listing Privilege (ILP), which allows the owners of rescued purebreds to participate in AKC companion events including obedience, agility, and tracking.

Shelters

Aussies of all ages find their way into humane societies for any number of reasons. Some are surrendered or abandoned by their owners. Others living in abusive conditions are confiscated by animal control officers and turned over to shelters. Lost or stray Australian Shepherds are often taken to a shelter by caring and compassionate residents. Many of these dogs are young to middle-aged. However, it is not unusual for older Australian Shepherds, some 7, 8, or 9 years old, to end up in an animal shelter. Shelter personnel screen all Aussies for temperament and placement before they become eligible for adoption. Many shelter dogs facing euthanasia are rescued by Aussie rescue organization volunteers and placed in foster homes for further adoption. Shelter dogs can and do make excellent companions, provided they are given the appropriate care and training.

THE PAPER TRAIL

When you purchase a purebred Australian Shepherd you should receive, at the very least, a bill of sale or sales contract, health records, pedigree, and registration application.

Bill of Sale

A bill of sale should include the puppy's name, sex, color, date whelped, date of sale, your name, address, and telephone number, as well as the name and address of the breeder, the purchase price of the puppy, and the date you bought and took possession. Often, a sales contract replaces a bill of sale, spelling out the entire purchase agreement, including any conditions or stipulations. For example,

if you purchased a conformation show, performance, or herding prospect, the contract may include breeder terms, such as stud rights on a male or puppies back from a female, and whether the dog is being sold outright or on a co-ownership basis. It may also state if a dog is to be spayed or neutered and, if so, a reasonable time frame in which it must be done. The contract should stipulate the conditions under which you are entitled to a full, partial, or zero refund for the dog. Do not assume the seller will automatically give you a free puppy if your dog develops problems.

Sales Contract

Sales contracts can include or exclude an enormous amount of information. Before signing on the dotted line, read all documents carefully, make sure you understand all the terms and conditions, and remember your Latin—*caveat emptor* (buyer beware!). When it doubt, it is always prudent to seek legal advice before signing contracts and legally binding documents.

Health Records

Most breeders do their best to eliminate genetic problems by having breeding stock tested for genetic problems and diseases. However, they cannot guarantee with absolute certainty that a dog will not develop a specific fault or disease. The best they can do is supply you with health records on your puppy's sire and dam, including hip certification by the Orthopedic Foundation for Animals (OFA) or the

Registering your Aussie with the AKC allows you to participate in many of their official activities.

University of Pennsylvania Hip Improvement Program (PennHIP), and complete eye examinations by a canine ophthalmologist and certification from the Canine Eye Registration Foundation (CERF). Certifications available on a young puppy are limited, but an 8-week-old Aussie can be examined to detect congenital heritable eye defects. A breeder should supply you with this documentation, too. This is not a lifetime certification, though. Annual examinations are recommended, because the health of the eyes can change from one year to the next.

Pedigree and Registration Application

You should receive registration papers that allow you to register the dog in your name and, at the minimum, a three-generation pedigree, which is your Aussie's family tree—a genetic blueprint that authenticates your dog's ancestry. However, it does not guarantee your Aussie has a shred of herding potential, is of show quality, or is free of inherited diseases or disorders.

BRINGING HOME YOUR AUSSIE

Once you have found the Aussie who is right for you, you should do certain things before bringing him home. While much of this information is geared toward preparing your home for a puppy, it applies equally to an adult dog. When you obtain an adult dog whose background and training are a bit sketchy, it is always a good idea to assume the dog has no training and begin his training as if he were a puppy.

Puppy Proofing

Puppy-proof your house *before* your new best friend arrives. This includes removing or putting out of reach anything your puppy is likely to seek out and destroy. Like toddlers, puppies will want to explore their surroundings and try to put everything in their mouth—whether it fits or not. Your puppy is too young to understand that your expensive leather heels are not for teething. Pick up shoes, books, magazines, and pillows. Put poisonous houseplants, prescription bottles, waste baskets, candy dishes, and so forth out of reach. Tuck electrical cords behind furniture, under rugs, or tape them to the baseboards. Many objects, such as shoelaces, buttons, socks, marbles, paperclips, and ripped up dolls, if swallowed, can cause life-threatening intestinal blockage and may require surgery to remove.

Rescue Organizations

- Aussie Rescue & Placement Helpline, Inc., (ARPH) is the official rescue organization of the Australian Shepherd Club of America (ASCA). Find them online at www.aussierescue.org.

- Second Time Around Aussie Rescue, Inc., (STAAR) is the official rescue organization of the United States Australian Shepherd Association (USASA). Find them online at www.staar.org.

Don't Forget Outside

Puppy-proof your yard, garden, and outdoor areas, too. Pick up hoses, sprinklers, poisonous plants, and lawn ornaments that your puppy will likely try to consume. Store containers of poisonous products—antifreeze, fertilizers, herbicides, and the like—on shelves and out of reach from your inquisitive puppy. Aussies are master escape artists, so make sure there are no holes in your fencing or broken gates that he is likely to escape through. If your property is not fenced, be sure your puppy is leashed each and every time he goes outdoors. He does not have the mental wherewithal to understand that the street is a dangerous place to be. It is your job to keep him safe.

AUSSIE ESSENTIALS

Basic essentials for your Australian Shepherd include a dog bed, collar and leash, crate, exercise pen, food and water bowls, identification, and an assortment of training toys and chew toys.

Beds

Your Aussie puppy will need a bed of his own, but it is best to hold off anything too expensive until he is well through the chewing stage. Aussies like to chew, and a tenacious chewer can turn a pricey canine bed into worthless scraps in just a few minutes. A large blanket or towel folded over several times, or a cozy fleece pad placed in his crate or exercise pen, will do the job for the first few months. They are easily cleaned in the washing machine, and therefore less likely to develop that distinctive doggie smell.

Collars and Leashes

Collars and leashes are essential equipment for every dog owner— but with a seemingly endless variety available, what's best for your Aussie?

Collars

Countless types and styles of collars are available, generally made of leather, nylon, cotton, or hemp. They also come in a variety of styles: buckle, harness, head halter, half-check, greyhound, choke chain, and martingale.

Every Australian Shepherd should wear a lightweight nylon or leather buckle collar with proper identification attached. This is his ticket home should he become lost or separated from you. Nylon collars work well with puppies because you will need to replace his collar several times before your puppy is fully grown. Nylon collars are relatively inexpensive and available at retail pet stores.

Leather collars are more expensive than nylon but well worth the investment for adult dogs, because they are softer yet sturdier and, given the right care, will last a lifetime. There are significant differences in the quality of leather collars, so if this is your preference, select a high-quality leather collar from a reputable manufacturer.

Several types of collars work by putting pressure on your dog's neck and throat, like choke chains, prong collars, and martingale collars. While it may be tempting to use these devices on an energetic and intense dog like an Australian Shepherd, these collars are best left to professionals. In the hands of an inexperienced person, these types of collars can cause serious damage to a dog's throat. Taking the time to train your Aussie to walk properly and not pull without these devices will be much more rewarding to you both.

If you have an Australian Shepherd who is a nuisance puller for whom your best training efforts have not succeeded, you might consider a head halter—depending on your level of patience. A head halter goes over your dog's face and applies pressure to the back of the neck rather than the front of the throat. While they can be very effective, most dogs are not used to this type of configuration, and it can require a great deal of preconditioning, patience, and diligence to make it a positive experience for your Australian Shepherd.

Harness

Some owners choose a harness for their dog. Keep in mind, a harness will not keep your Australian Shepherd from pulling, but it will take the pressure off his trachea. A variety of models are available in different shapes, sizes, and materials. Seek professional advice to correctly fit your Australian Shepherd with a harness.

Leashes

Like collars, leashes come in a variety of choices, but when all is said and done choosing a leash is usually a matter of personal preference. Nylon leashes are lightweight and relatively inexpensive, and it never hurts to have an extra one in the car, motor home, or around the house. Available in every color of the rainbow, nylon

Make sure the collar fits properly.

Leash Tip

Retractable leads are ideal for teaching and reinforcing the Come command.

leashes can be personalized with your name and telephone number, but they are not always the best choice for medium or large dogs because they are hard on your hands and can slice your fingers to the bone should your Aussie lunge or give a good pull.

Leather leashes are quite a bit more costly but well worth the investment when you own an Australian Shepherd. Unlike nylon leashes, leather leashes are gentler on your hands, which is important because you'll be using the leash a lot—and the more you use it, the softer and more pliable it becomes. A good quality, well cared for leather leash will be around long after your Aussie has settled into his golden years.

When purchasing a nylon or leather leash, buy one that is appropriate for the size of your dog. A lightweight nylon leash suitable for an adult Bichon Frise may work temporarily on an Aussie puppy, but it will do you no good on an adult Aussie. Generally, a 5/8- or 3/4-inch (1.6- or 1.9-cm) wide leather or nylon leash will provide sufficient strength and control as your Aussie grows bigger and stronger.

Retractable leads are designed to extend and retract at the touch of a button. They allow you to give your Aussie plenty of distance on walks without carrying a long line that can get tangled, dragged through the mud, or wrapped around bushes. A retractable lead that extends to 16 feet (5 m), or more, allows your Aussie plenty of privacy to do his business, sniff, and explore myriad sights and smells. A finger brake button allows you to stop your dog at any time. If you go this route, invest in a good-quality retractable lead designed specifically for strong, medium-sized dogs; the proper leash should last a lifetime.

Crate

A crate is an absolute necessity if you own an Aussie. Crates come in different shapes, sizes, and materials, each offering its own advantages. Folding wire crates provide good air circulation and help keep dogs cool when temperatures are high, and a variety of crate covers turn any wire crate into a secure den with protection from the elements. Other crate

Fitting a Collar

A buckle collar should be neither too tight nor too loose. Ideally, it should fit around your Aussie's neck with enough room to fit two fingers between his neck and the collar. It should not be so tight as to restrict his breathing or cause coughing. Nor should it be so loose that it slips over his head. When too loose, the collar can easily snag on objects, such as shrubbery, a fence post, or another dog's tooth or paw, causing the dog to panic and inadvertently hang himself. Equally important, growing puppies quickly outgrow their collars. Be sure to check collar size frequently on puppies. Left unchecked, a collar that is too small can become imbedded in a dog's neck, causing serious health issues. Check your dog's collar regularly to ensure it is not frayed or worn.

types include nylon or heavy-duty, high-impact plastic kennels that meet domestic and international requirements for airline travel. Folding crates such as those made by Nylabone have the added value and convenience of being easy to store away when not in use.

When shopping for a crate, purchase one that is big enough for your Aussie when he is full grown. Ideally, it should be big enough for your adult Aussie to stand up, turn around, and stretch out while lying down. If the crate is too big, it defeats the purpose of providing the security of a den. If it is too small, your Aussie will be cramped and uncomfortable, and this is neither fair nor humane. During the housetraining stage, a crate that is too large allows a puppy to use one end for sleeping and the other end as a bathroom, which defeats the crate's usefulness as a housetraining tool. Some crates come equipped with a divider panel that allows you to adjust the crate space accordingly. This option allows you to block off a portion of the crate for housetraining purposes, and can take your Aussie from the puppy stage through housetraining and into adulthood without the expense of purchasing multiple size crates.

Exercise Pen

Like a crate, an exercise pen is indispensable for raising a well-behaved puppy. They are ideal for placing anywhere you need a temporary kennel area, such as the kitchen or family room. Like a crate, a pen is essential for safely confining your Aussie when you cannot give him your undivided attention, such as when you are eating, working on the computer, talking on the telephone, or doing the laundry.

If you place the exercise pen in the kitchen area—or wherever your family tends to congregate—your puppy can get used to many sights, sounds, and smells from the safety of his exercise pen. Most owners prefer the kitchen area, because kitchens tend to have washable floors and can easily be cleaned and disinfected if your puppy has an accident.

Food and Water Bowls

Your dog might consider these the most important items on your list of supplies for him. After all, mealtimes are some of a dog's best times, and you want to be sure your puppy or dog has bowls for both food and water.

Like other doggy essentials, there are plenty of bowls to choose from, and you can have a lot of fun with the selection. The bowls you

Choosing a Crate

If you aren't sure what type of crate to purchase for your Aussie, ask a breeder, veterinarian, or knowledgeable dog person to recommend a size and style.

select should be easy to clean, made of material that is not potentially harmful, and they should not slide when placed on the floor.

To meet these criteria, focus on stainless steel or heavy ceramic bowls—as long as the ceramic is finished with nontoxic glaze. Stainless steel is especially easy to clean, and most models come with rubberized bottoms to keep them from sliding. Plastic bowls are inexpensive, but they are not the best choice for the tenacious chewer, who could ingest or choke on shredded pieces. Also, plastic is not as easily sanitized as stainless steel and can harbor bacteria.

A bowl of clean, fresh water must be available for your Aussie at all times. Rinse the bowl and refill it several times a day, and thoroughly clean it at least once a day. Your dog's food bowl should be cleaned before and after his regular meals.

Identification

Even the most conscientious owner can experience the nightmare of a lost dog—that's why it's crucial that your Aussie is properly identified.

An exercise pen can help keep your puppy enclosed.

ID Tags

Your Aussie must have an I.D. tag that includes, at the minimum, your name and telephone number. These tags are relatively inexpensive and well worth the investment because they are your dog's ticket home should he become lost or separated. Readily available at retail pet outlets, mail order catalogs, and online vendors, tags come in a variety of shapes, sizes, colors, and materials. They easily attach to your dog's buckle collar with an S clip or good-quality split ring. You can even find nameplates that attach directly to your dog's collar, which eliminate the unmistakable, not to mention frequently annoying, jingling noise produced by multiple tags dangling from a dog's collar.

Microchipping

Until recently, tattooing was the most widely used method of permanently identifying an animal. Modern technology has given pet owners the latest in identification options—a silicon microchip about the size of a grain of rice, that is painlessly inserted under your Aussie's skin. The microchip contains an unalterable identification number that is recorded on a central database along with your name, address, and telephone number. The microchip is scanned, and the identification number is read via a hand-held electronic scanner. A universal scanner can detect and read the numbers of all major brands of microchips. A microchip will not do your Aussie any good if it is not registered. So don't forget the paperwork!

Several state and national registries are available for registering and storing your contact information.

Australian Shepherds like to cool off by jumping into a trough of water or kiddy pool, or even standing in a bucket of water. Having one readily available for your Aussie will ensure he has plenty of opportunity to cool off and prevent him from overheating.

Toys

Aussies, like all dogs, not only enjoy chewing, they *need* to chew—especially puppies, who will experience teething as their baby teeth erupt and fall out. Again, a vast and endlessly entertaining selection of dog toys is available, and you and your Australian Shepherd can have a lot of fun selecting favorites. The healthiest and longest-lasting selections, however, will be toys made for your Aussie's body type and chewing power. Hard nylon and rubber toys are made for real gnawing and gnashing. They exercise your dog's teeth and gums, promoting oral health while relieving the need to chew. Nylabone makes some toys that are suitable for an Aussie's size and chewing power.

Be careful with plush toys that contain squeakers or noise-makers. Tenacious Aussies will chew right through the material and may swallow the squeaker, which could become lodged in their throat.

Many kinds of edible chews and dog toys provide nutritional enhancement or breath fresheners. Most are strong enough for your Australian Shepherd to get a good chew out of before breaking into bits that can be eaten. These should not be substitutes for the more long-lasting chew toys, but they make an enjoyable break for your dog.

TRAVELING WITH YOUR AUSTRALIAN SHEPHERD

Australian Shepherds love a good road trip. Most Aussies are quite adaptable and make wonderful travelers, but do not wait until you are on the road to discover yours is not! Ideally, it is best to accustom your Aussie to traveling while he is young and more receptive to new adventures.

By Car

For most Aussies, riding in the family car is part of their everyday life and as natural as eating, sleeping, or herding sheep. One of the best ways to accustom your new Aussie to traveling is to put him in his crate and take him everywhere (weather providing, of course). Take him for a ride to the post office, bank, and grocery store and to visit your friends and family. Make the experience fun by giving him treats and telling him he's great!

Carsickness

Aussies who have never been in a car, or who have developed phobias, are often anxious or apprehensive about car rides. Some dog's drool, shake, and even vomit. For dogs who have true motion sickness, which is normally associated with an inner ear problem, medications are available and can be used under the supervision of a veterinarian. Carsickness, on the other hand, is usually associated with fear or an apprehension of the car noise and movement, a response to the dog's inability to control his circumstances, or a traumatic experience in a car or at the journey's end, such as an unpleasant experience at a vet's office or obedience class.

If your Aussie has problems riding in the car, begin reconditioning him by simply sitting in the car without the motor running while you verbally praise him for being brave and reward him with tasty treats.

Dog harnesses that attach to your car's seatbelt are available for travel.

What to Pack for Your Australian Shepherd

When traveling, do not forget to pack a few necessities for your dog:

- Your Aussie's current health certificate and rabies inoculation.
- Current photographs of your dog, to be used for identification should he become lost.
- An extra leash, collar, and set of ID tags.
- An adequate supply of food, water, and feeding dishes.
- A pooper-scooper, paper towels, or plastic bags for picking up after your dog.
- Medications and prescriptions.
- Chew toys, bones, tug toys, balls, and the like.
- A favorite blanket or bed.
- An adequate supply of doggie towels for quick cleanups, in the event your dog gets wet, dirty, or injured

Progress to sitting in the car with the motor running. Again, verbally praise and reward him with yummy tidbits. The next step is short, fun trips around the block, to the post office, bank, and so forth. Each time, gradually increase the distance, always making the experience fun and positive. Put a favorite blanket, toy, or treat in his crate to keep him comfy and occupied.

Aussies are awesome traveling companions, and there's no limit to the fun you can have exploring together. So it's well worth the training to help your dog overcome his fear of riding in a car.

Over-the-counter products are available to help calm your Aussie. In severe cases, your veterinarian can prescribe a stronger, anti-anxiety medication. Always consult a veterinarian before giving your Aussie tranquilizers, aspirins, or medications prescribed for humans.

Remember, traveling with an Aussie is not unlike traveling with toddlers and small children. Make frequent pit stops a priority so that your dog can relieve himself, stretch his legs, and burn off some pent-up energy.

By Air

Dogs traveling by air are protected by U.S. Department of Agriculture (USDA) regulations. That in itself does not guarantee your pet will be safe flying the friendly skies. However, there are safety regulations and precautions to help minimize potential dangers, including the following:

- Dogs must be at least 8 weeks old and be weaned prior to traveling.

- A licensed veterinarian must examine your dog and issue a health certificate within 10 days of traveling.
- Dogs must travel in airline-approved crates that meet stringent USDA regulations for size, strength, sanitation, and ventilation. Your Aussie may be refused a boarding pass if his kennel does not meet the government's requirements.
- Dogs flying outside the continental United States may be subjected to quarantine regulations.

Regulations vary from airline to airline, so it is important to always plan ahead. Not all airlines accept dogs , and many limit the number of dogs accepted on each flight. Call the airlines well in advance of your travel plans to schedule flights. Ideally, when booking a flight try to:

- Book nonstop flights during the middle of the week, avoiding holiday or weekend travel.
- Avoid layovers and plane changes, if possible.
- During warm weather, choose flights early in the morning or late in the evening.
- In cooler months, choose midday flights.

Specific regulations for national and international air travel are available on the USDA webpage: http://www.aphis.usda.gov/ac.

Hotel or Motel

If you plan to stay at a hotel or motel, call ahead to be sure they accept dogs. Not all hotels and motels accept dogs—even well-behaved Australian Shepherds. Some facilities allow dogs in the rooms, but may require the dog be crated. Some larger hotels provide kennel facilities. Many require a refundable pet deposit or a nonrefundable pet fee.

Be a good ambassador for the Aussie breed—as well as all dogs— by following hotel and motel rules, including never leaving an unattended dog in the room. An otherwise calm Aussie may become anxious in unfamiliar surroundings. He may chew furniture, shred pillows, urinate, defecate, or annoy other visitors with his barking and whining. His natural guarding instinct can be disastrous if he tries to nip the maid. Without exception, always clean up after your dog and deposit any messes in designated trash bins.

Auto clubs usually list approved lodgings that accept dogs, and a number of guidebooks list regional and national dog-friendly motels and hotels.

Campgrounds

Like hotels and motels, not all public or private parks and campgrounds allow dogs. Most recreational vehicle clubs provide directories that include a park's pet policy. However, these policies are subject to change, so it is highly advisable to call ahead. Be sure to follow park rules, and never allow your Australian Shepherd to intrude on other campers or their animals. Never leave your Australian Shepherd unattended or tied out where he can be teased, stolen, or attacked by another dog or wild animals.

WHEN YOU CAN'T TAKE YOUR AUSSIE WITH YOU

Family emergencies, unexpected business trips, and intemperate weather may exclude your best friend from your travel plans. Whatever the reason, occasions may arise when you need to leave your Aussie for a few days or a few weeks. Yes, it's heartbreaking, but a few options are available to give you some peace of mind.

Camping can be a great vacation for the whole family, including your Aussie.

Boarding Facilities

Boarding facilities have come a long way in the last 10 or 15 years. Many are now designed with the discriminating pet owner in mind, and they provide a variety of services including training, daily exercise, and grooming. Some facilities provide video cameras that allow you to view your Aussie via a laptop or PC.

Your Aussies' physical safety and emotional well being are paramount. Here are some tips for reducing you and your dog's stress by choosing the best facility:

- Visit and tour the entire facility. A clean and inviting reception area does not guarantee clean kennel runs. If the proprietors do not want you touring the facility—hightail it to the nearest exit.
- Check the cleanliness of the kennels, runs, and exercise areas. Make sure they are free of debris and excrement, and cleaned and disinfected between boarders. Check if the kennel or exercise area smells.
- Check the security of the facility. It should be completely fenced; the kennels and exercise yards should have good latches; with sturdy fences at least 6 feet (1.8 m) high.
- Find out if your Aussie will be boarded indoors or out (or a combination of the two). The indoor facilities should be heated, and the outdoor facilities protected from the weather.
- Look at what your Aussie be sleeping on, and if you need to bring his bed or favorite blanket.
- If you have several Aussies, ask if you can kennel them together, and what, if any, additional costs this might incur.
- Find out how frequently and for how long your Aussie will be walked or exercised. A good boarding kennel will have someone interact or play with him, and not just leave him unattended in an exercise yard.
- It can be extremely dangerous and stressful to have your Aussie housed with other dogs, so make sure he won't have a kennelmate.
- Ask about the facility's veterinarian, and if there is a 24-hour emergency clinic nearby.
- Find out their admission and pick-up hours, and what happens if your return is delayed.
- Get a list of required vaccinations.

Once you have decided on a facility, book early. Many facilities are booked months in advance, especially during the holidays. Always leave special pet-care instructions, your itinerary, and numbers to contact you or a trusted friend or relative in the event of an emergency.

Pet Sitters

If boarding your Aussie is out of the question, consider a pet sitter. Yes, he'll still miss you, but there's a good chance he will be less stressed in the comfort of his own home, surrounded by your scent and his prized possessions. You may be lucky enough to have a responsible neighbor, trusted friend, or relative you can rely on to stop by several times a day but, if not, seek out the services of a professional pet sitter.

Pet sitters either stay at your home while you are gone or stop in during the day to feed, exercise, and check on your dog. Ask your dog-owing friends, local veterinarians, trainers, or groomers for a referral.

If you choose the pet sitting route, have the pet sitter come to your home for an interview:

- Are they professional? Did they show up on time?
- How do they relate to your Aussie?
- How much experience do they have?
- Will they be able to recognize if your dog is sick or having a problem?
- If they are not staying at your house, how often will they come by?
- Will they play with your Aussie? Talk to him? Kiss him? Love him?
- Are they licensed? Bonded? Insured?

Doggy Day Care

Doggy day cares are similar to day care centers for human children, but with a twist. They are for dogs! If you want your Aussie to play and interact with other dogs while you slave away at work, doggie day care may be your cup of tea.

Day care centers vary in their appearance, amenities, and cost. Some resemble park-like atmospheres with trees, park benches, kiddy pools, and playground equipment. Some facilities provide spa-like amenities and lavish the dogs with attention, including hydro-baths, nail trims, and massages.

To find the right day care facility for your Australian Shepherd, consider the same points as you would for a boarding facility.

FEEDING
Your Australian Shepherd

Good nutrition is really important to your Australian Shepherd's well being. A good diet, along with exercise, is perhaps the single most important contributor to a healthy skin and coat, strong bones and ligaments, and optimum health and longevity. Feeding your Aussie a high-quality, well-balanced diet also gives him the energy he needs to get through his day, be it herding sheep or tussling with kids. That said, it's prudent to stick with a diet designed specifically for canines, because a number of human foods can cause life-threatening medical problems for dogs. While a stroll down the pet food aisle can seem more intimidating than computer science, feeding a well-balanced diet doesn't require a Ph.D. in nutrition. All it really requires is a fundamental understanding of nutrients and how they work, a keen observation of your Aussie and whether his diet is agreeing with him, and, finally, the ability to look beyond the multimillion-dollar ad campaigns.

BASIC NUTRITION

All dogs are not created equal when it comes to nutrition. Some Aussies have allergies to different food sources—such as beef, chicken, or fish—which can cause an array of troubles, including scratching and intestinal gas. Others are sensitive or intolerant to poor-quality ingredients and grain-based diets. Identifying food allergies can be difficult and usually requires a trip to a veterinary dermatologist.

To help your Aussie's complex system run efficiently, it is important to find the diet that provides the correct balance of nutrients for his individual requirements. What works for one Aussie may not work for another because a dog's nutritional needs will change depending on his age, environment, housing conditions, exposure to heat or cold, overall health, and the emotional and physical demands placed on him. Some Aussies are constantly in motion, and the more active the dog, the more energy he burns. As a result, active Aussies require a higher intake of nutrients to fuel their bodies. An Aussie who works full-time in a herding environment requires more calories than the family pet who runs and plays with the kids for an hour each day. If your senior Aussie's primary job is guarding the couch, he will not require as many calories as an agility competitor. A pregnant or lactating bitch's nutritional requirements will differ from that of a 10-year-old spayed Australian Shepherd.

Your Aussie's diet is likely to change several times over the course of his lifetime. However, the nuts and bolts of canine nutrition remain the same. There are six basic elements of nutrition: carbohydrates, fats, minerals, proteins, vitamins, and water.

Carbohydrates

Dogs are omnivorous animals, meaning they eat both animal and vegetable foods, and they get most of their energy from carbohydrates. Carbohydrates are the fuel for your Australian Shepherd's body. Scientific research indicates that up to 50 percent of an adult dog's diet can come from carbohydrates. They are often referred to as *protein-sparing* nutrients because the action of carbohydrates (and fats) in providing energy allows protein to be used in its own unique role.

Soluble carbohydrates consist mainly of starches and sugars and are easily digested. Insoluble carbohydrates, better known as *fiber*, resist enzymatic digestion in the small intestine. Fiber, while important to the overall process, is not an essential nutrient.

Carbohydrates are introduced in the diet primarily through vegetable matter—legumes and cereal grains, such as rice, wheat, corn, barley, and oats. Unused carbohydrates are stored in the body as converted fat, and as glycogen in the muscles and liver. In the absence of adequate carbohydrates, your Aussie's system is able to utilize fat and protein as a form of energy. However, protein is less efficient because the body does not make a specialized storage form of protein as it does for fats and carbohydrates. When protein is used as an energy source—rather than to do its unique job of building muscle,

It is important to find the diet that provides the correct balance of nutrients for his individual requirements.

regulating body functions, and so forth—a dog's body must dismantle his valuable tissue proteins and use them for energy.

Fats

Fats and oils are the most concentrated sources of food energy in your Aussie's diet. Fats account for approximately 2.25 times more metabolizable energy—the amount of energy in the food actually available to the dog—than do carbohydrates or proteins. Fats play an important role in contributing to your dog's healthy skin and coat and aid in the absorption, transport, and storage of fat-soluble vitamins. Fats also increase the palatability of foods, but they contain more than twice the calories of proteins and carbohydrates. Just as in your own diet, fats in your Aussie's diet should be regulated. Dogs seldom develop the cardiovascular problems that humans do, but consuming too much fat can result in excess calorie intake, which is not good for your Australian Shepherd's health or waistline.

A Mineral Don't

You should never attempt to supplement minerals in your Australian Shepherd's diet without professional advice from a veterinarian.

Minerals

Minerals are not a source of energy, but they are important in the overall nutritional equation because they help regulate your Aussie's complex system and are crucial components in energy metabolism. Minerals are classified as macro minerals or micro minerals depending on their concentration in the body. Micro minerals, or trace elements, include iodine, iron, copper, cobalt, zinc, manganese, molybdenum, fluorine, and chromium, which dogs need in very small amounts. Macro minerals are needed in large quantities and include sodium, potassium, magnesium, calcium, and phosphorous.

Essential nutrients are those that your Aussie must obtain from food because his body cannot make them in sufficient quantity to meet physiological needs. If dogs get too much or too little of a specific mineral in their diets, it can upset the delicate balance and cause serious health problems, including tissue damage, convulsions, increased heart rate, and anemia.

Protein

Proteins are compounds of carbon, hydrogen, oxygen, and nitrogen atoms arranged into a string of amino acids—much like the pearls on a necklace. Amino acids are the building blocks of life, because they produce vital proteins that build strong muscles, ligaments, organs, bones, teeth, and coat. Protein also defends the body against disease, and it's critical when it comes to the repair and maintenance of all the body's tissue, hormones, enzymes, electrolyte balances, and antibodies.

There are ten essential amino acids that your Aussie's body cannot make on its own or make in sufficient quantities. These amino acids must be obtained through his diet. To make protein, a cell must have all the needed amino acids available simultaneously because the body makes complete proteins only. If one amino acid is missing, the other amino acids cannot form a partial protein. If complete proteins are not formed, it reduces and limits the body's ability to grow and repair tissue.

Vitamins

A dog's body does not extract usable energy from vitamins, but they are essential helpers in the metabolic processes. Vitamins are vital to your Aussie's health and available in food sources, but they can be easily destroyed in the cooking and processing of commercial dog foods. Certain vitamins depend on one another, and nearly every action in a dog's body requires the assistance of vitamins. Vitamin deficiencies or excesses can lead to serious health problems, such as anorexia, artery and vein degeneration, dehydration, muscle weakness, and impairment of motor control and balance.

Vitamins fall into two categories: water-soluble (B-complex and vitamin C) and fat-soluble (A, D, E, and K). Unlike humans, dogs can make vitamin C from glucose so they do not need to acquire it in their diet. All other water-soluble vitamins must be replenished on a regular basis through diet. Fat-soluble vitamins are absorbed and stored in the body, which makes oversupplementation potentially dangerous. Seek your veterinarian's advice and read as much as you can before supplementing your dog's food.

Provide plenty of fresh water for your Aussie.

Water

One seldom thinks of water as an essential nutrient. However, it is the single most important nutrient needed to sustain your four-legged friend's health. Water regulates your Aussie's body temperature, plays an important part in supporting metabolic reactions, and acts as the transportation system, so to speak, that allows blood to carry vital nutritional materials to the cells and remove waste products from your dog's system.

The amount of water a dog needs to consume daily will vary from dog to dog depending on growth, stress, environment, activity, and age. Your Aussie's need for water increases as he expends more energy during work, exercise, play, or training because dissipation of excess heat from his body is accomplished largely by the evaporation of water through panting. Plus, the warmer the weather, the more water he's going to need to consume. If your Aussie eats primarily dry dog food, he will also need access to fresh water to help aid in digestion.

Rather than trying to estimate your Aussie's daily water requirement, it is best to provide him with access to an abundant supply of fresh, cool drinking water at all times. When dogs have free access to water, they will normally drink enough to maintain the proper balance of body fluids. If you have less than desirable city water or are concerned about fluoride, chlorine, or lead in your water supply, consider a filtration system or purchasing bottled water for your Aussie.

Contaminated Water

Infectious agents and diseases, such as leptospirosis, *Giardia*, and *E. coli* can be transmitted through contaminated water. To reduce the risk of disease, do not allow your Aussie to drink from puddles, streams, or ponds, because the water could be contaminated with parasites that could make him ill.

FOOD CHOICES FOR YOUR AUSTRALIAN SHEPHERD

When it comes to feeding your Australian Shepherd, a number of different options are available. From convenient commercial foods to healthy home cooked meals, the most important thing to remember is to find a diet that works for you and your Aussie. Make sure you speak to your vet before making any drastic changes to your dog's diet.

Commercial Diets

Commercial diets are undoubtedly the most convenient foods to buy, store, and use. They are readily available and, when compared to homemade diets, they are definitely less time consuming. Most major dog-food manufacturers, and a number of veterinary hospitals, have invested enormous sums of money in researching and studying the nutritional requirements of dogs at different stages of life. As a result, they are quite knowledgeable about what constitutes good canine nutrition.

Keep in mind that the commercial dog food industry is a multibillion-dollar-a-year business. Advertising experts

Premium Foods

There is no substitute for good nutrition. For maximum health and longevity, your Aussie must be properly fed and cared for throughout his life. Buying a premium food is more expensive than a bargain or generic brand food but, in the long run, it makes good nutritional and economic sense. Across the board, premium foods tend to be nutritionally complete, meaning they have all the required nutrients in balanced proportion, so your Aussie is getting adequate amounts of all required nutrients. Premium foods are also developed to provide optimal nutrition for dogs during different stages of life, such as puppy, maintenance, active, and senior diets. The initial investment for a premium food is a bit higher on a per weight basis, but because they tend to be higher in digestibility and nutrient availability, less food is required per serving.

spend a significant amount of time researching, developing, and marketing products in a manner to convince you to buy a particular brand. This is not necessarily bad, but it is important to remember if you are choosing a food because of the creative advertisements and fancy packaging, rather than the nutritional requirements of your dog.

Commercial foods tend to be classified into food types: dry, canned, and semi-moist. Frozen and dehydrated foods also are becoming increasingly popular in the competitive food market.

Canned Foods

Canned foods are mostly water—approximately 75 percent. They contain more meat than a dry diet and little to no grain.

Dry Food

Dry foods, commonly called "kibble," contain between 6 to 10 percent moisture (water) and a high percentage of carbohydrates in the form of grains.

Semi-Moist Foods

Semi-moist foods are often shaped into patties and come in a prepackaged size convenient for feeding. They are generally marketed in sealed and resealable pouches. They are 25 to 35 percent water. Ingredients can include fresh or frozen animal tissues, cereal grains, fats, and simple sugars. Semi-moist foods also contain propylene glycol, which is an odorless, tasteless, slightly syrupy liquid used to make antifreeze and de-icing products. Propylene glycol is generally recognized as safe by the U.S. Food and Drug Administration (FDA) for use in dog food and other animal feeds. It is used to absorb extra water and maintain moisture, and as a solvent for food coloring and flavor.

Food Comparisons

For a look at the advantages and disadvantages of food choices for your Aussie, see pages 82-83.

Noncommercial Diets

Although commercial diets provide your dog with a balanced, no-fuss diet, you may opt to feed a homemade or raw diet. Before jumping in, carefully consider the pros and cons of both.

Bones and Raw Food Diet (BARF)

It is not difficult to find proponents and opponents on both sides of the controversial issue of whether a BARF diet is best for dogs. Ask a dozen people, and each is sure to have a different opinion. Essentially, some owners believe that raw foods are more suitable for their dog than highly processed foods. They believe drying, freezing, heating, or canning food robs it of its nutritional components. It appears that by returning to a more *natural* lifestyle and feeding a *pure* diet, they hope to mimic or replicate what wild dogs might have eaten long ago.

Two challenges arise with this type of diet: First, it is difficult to find a good source of healthy raw meat and bones, and then achieve the correct balance of nutrients—water, vitamins, minerals, protein, carbohydrates, fats—in the right amounts, and do so on a routine basis. Second, dogs who eat bones, particularly chicken and turkey bones, are highly susceptible to choking or damaging their stomachs. Both these situations can be life-threatening. In addition, parasites are a concern because dogs, like humans, are susceptible to internal parasites, bacteria, and food-borne illnesses caused by raw meat, poultry, eggs, and unprocessed milk.

Feeding a raw food and bones diet works for some owners.

Feeding a non-commercial diet to your pet allows you to control the ingredients.

However, feeding this type of diet should be undertaken only after a great deal of research. It is highly recommended you work closely with a veterinarian or certified canine nutritionist.

Homemade Diets

Let's face it, unless you are schooled in canine nutrition, and you have an abundance of time and energy on your hands, feeding a homemade diet is easier said than done. Preparing your Aussie's food from scratch is a great idea—in theory. After all, who doesn't want the best for her dog? Most owners want to feed foods free of preservatives, additives, and who knows what else.

Truth be told, homemade diets are a time-consuming, labor-intensive, expensive, and complicated process. It is tricky, albeit not impossible, to prepare a canine diet on a routine daily basis that is complete and balanced and contains the proper ratio of nutrients. Do you know the calcium/phosphorous ratio in the diet you are preparing? The nutritional value of raw ingredients will fluctuate depending on their sources, and supplementing with vitamins and minerals is usually necessary. However, that can be harmful to your dog if too much or too little or the wrong combinations of supplements are used. One suggestion is to whirl all the food ingredients, supplements, treats, snacks, and so forth, into a blender and have the sample professionally analyzed. This will tell you if your Aussie is really getting a balanced diet. You might be surprised at the results—not to mention the costly invoice!

The bottom line is, when you choose to feed a homemade diet, you assume full responsibility for the nutritional status of your Aussie. If

Scheduled versus Free-Feeding

Scheduled feeding is probably best for your Aussie. Feed your puppy at regular times, and whatever food is left after 15 minutes, pick up and throw away. This regimen helps your puppy establish a regular routine of eating and eliminating, which helps speed up the housetraining process. Designated feeding times also help with the bonding process. Your puppy learns food comes from you—the pack leader. It also helps to avoid obesity in your puppy. Juvenile obesity increases the number of fat cells in a puppy and predisposes him to obesity for the rest of his life.

Free-feeding, which is putting the food out, leaving it all day, and allowing your puppy to eat at his leisure, does not establish a set schedule for feeding and eliminating. Leaving food out also attracts ants, birds, squirrels, stray cats, and other critters. Some Aussies are able to regulate their food intake, but most Aussies will eat until they make themselves sick and then happily start all over again. When food is perpetually available, some dogs develop the annoying and potential dangerous habit of food-bowl guarding. Finally, if you have multiple dogs, feeding them separately in crates, kennels or at opposite sides of the house while they eat is recommended. Otherwise, you will not know for certain if your puppy is eating or the other dogs are eating for him. Even the best of friends have been known to squabble over food.

this is what you decide to do, consult with a veterinarian or certified veterinary nutritionist before proceeding

FEEDING YOUR PUPPY

An Aussie puppy has gigantic nutritional demands. In addition to the fact that a puppy spends a significant part of his day playing, which requires a lot of calories, his body is growing rapidly. His system is building strong muscles, bones, and vital organs, and establishing a resistance to disease. As a result, for the first 12 months of his life, he needs a specially formulated growth food designed exclusively for his demanding energy and nutritional needs.

How Often?

A growing Aussie needs about twice as many calories per pound of body weight as an adult Aussie. Since puppies have small stomachs, they also need to be fed smaller amounts of food three or four times a day until they are about 6 months old. From 6 months to 1 year of age and thereafter, feed your Aussie two times a day—once in the morning and again in the evening.

How Much?

Your Aussie's growth rate and appetite are primarily dictated by his genetics, which varies from puppy to puppy, so feeding the correct amount can be a bit tricky. The feeding guidelines on puppy foods are just that—guidelines. They are not etched in stone, and many dog food manufacturers tend to be overly generous with their proportions. Your veterinarian can help you determine the proper amount to feed.

Switching Foods

For the first few days after bringing your precious pooch home, continue feeding the same type and brand of puppy food he has been eating, provided he has been eating a well-balanced, good-quality puppy food. Depending on where and from whom you purchase your Australian Shepherd, this may or may not be the case.

If you intend to switch foods, do so slowly to prevent intestinal upset. Veterinarians recommend switching foods over the course of 7 to 10 days to prevent upset stomachs, vomiting, loose stool, or constipation. To do this, make a mixture of 75 percent old food and 25 percent new food. Feed this mixture for 3 or 4 days. Then make

Prescription Diets

Prescription diets are special-formula diets prepared by dog-food manufacturers and normally available only through a licensed veterinarian. They are designed to meet the special medical needs of certain dogs, such as low-protein and -mineral diets for kidney disease; low-protein, -magnesium, -calcium, and -phosphorous for bladder stones; lamb-and-rice-based diets for food-induced allergies; and low-calorie foods for weight-reduction diets.

Is Your Aussie "Active"?

Consider your Aussie active if he gets at least one hour of continuous exercise a day.

a mixture of 50 percent old food and 50 percent new food. Feed this mixture for 3 or 4 days. Then make a mixture of 25 percent old food and 75 percent new food. Feed this mixture for 3 or 4 days. Then you can start feeding 100 percent new food.

FEEDING YOUR ADULT

Different breeds of dogs reach maturity at different ages. As a general rule, smaller breeds tend to reach adulthood sooner than do large-breed dogs. Your Aussie will most likely reach adulthood around 12 months of age. That said, the age of maturity varies from Aussie to Aussie, with some Aussies reaching maturity sooner or later than others.

Adult foods, often called *maintenance diets*, are specially designed foods that satisfy the energy and nutritional needs of adult dogs who have reached maturity. These diets are designed to provide the proper quantities of nutrients to support a mature Australian Shepherd's lifestyle. Aussies who are very active, under physical or emotional stress, and lactating bitches have different nutrient requirements than do the average canine couch potato. Your veterinarian can help you determine when and what type of adult food to choose.

How Often?

Most experts recommend feeding an adult dog twice a day—once in the morning and again in the early evening. As with puppies, pick up any food left after 15 minutes and toss it.

How Much?

Generally speaking, most premium dog foods contain between 350 and 550 calories per cup, and most active adult Aussies require about 2 cups per day (1 cup in the morning, and 1 cup in the evening). This is a guideline, and the amount your adult Aussie requires depends on his exercise level and individual metabolism. Many dog food manufacturers are overly generous when it comes to the feeding guidelines on dog food packages. If your Aussie is packing on the pounds, cut back slightly on his food and/or treat intake, or increase his activity level—or both. When in doubt, your veterinarian can help you determine the correct amount to feed.

FEEDING YOUR SENIOR

Aussies age at different rates. Determining if and when you should begin feeding a senior food depends on your individual dog. It is impossible to arbitrarily set an "old-age" age. You cannot randomly say that Australian Shepherds are old at 8 or 9 years of age. Like humans, dogs age differently depending on their genetics and lifestyle.

A good rule of thumb used by many veterinarians is to divide the average lifespan of your Aussie into thirds. When your Aussie is in the last third of his life, he is usually considered an older dog. Using that simplified mathematical equation, the average Aussie is considered a senior around 9 or 10 years of age. Again, there are exceptions to every rule and some Aussies remain physically and cognitively young at 12, 13, or 14 years of age.

Older dogs usually require a diet that is still complete and well balanced, yet lower in calories, protein, and fat. In some instances, you may be able to feed your Australian Shepherd his regular adult food but in smaller quantities. Or, you may need to switch to a diet designed specifically for senior dogs.

Special Concerns for Seniors

Because older dogs do not normally get as much exercise as their younger counterparts, losing weight can be difficult for them. Maintaining a sensible weight throughout your Aussie's entire life is one of the most important and humane things you can do to help retain good health and increase the quality and length of his life. Knowing this ahead of time, take precautions that do not allow your Aussie to become overweight at any stage of his life.

On the other side of the spectrum, older dogs occasionally will go off of their food, meaning they lose interest in it, and they may choose to eat only once a day. If your Aussie is losing weight, or if his eating habits have changed, it is important that a veterinarian exam him to rule out any possible disease problems. Because dogs age at different rates, work closely with a veterinarian as your Aussie begins to enter his senior years. Your veterinarian can help you determine the

How much you feed your adult Aussie depends on his activity level.

nutritional and supplemental needs of your Australian Shepherd in this stage of his life.

OBESITY

As a rule, obesity in Aussies is no more common than in any other breed. Working Australian Shepherds are seldom, if ever, overweight. After all, they spend the majority of their time on the go—working livestock, patrolling their territory, running, jumping, and frequently being silly. That's not to say Aussies don't get fat. More than a few Aussies—even competition Aussies—are tilting the scales, and they shouldn't be.

Regardless of breed, dogs who are overfed—be it too much kibble or too many table scraps and high-fat snacks—are likely to become overweight or obese. Some dogs, regardless of the breed, are "easy keepers"—meaning their weight seldom fluctuates. Others gain weight with just a few extra kibbles and snacks each day.

Like humans, dogs who are carrying around extra pounds are subject to serious health issues including diabetes, increased blood pressure, congestive heart failure, and digestive disorders. Fat works as an insulator, which is great if you're a hibernating bear, but too much fat is going to wreak havoc with your Aussie's internal and external parts. For starters, extra fat restricts the expansion of your Aussie's lungs, making breathing difficult. Overweight Aussies are less capable of regulating their body temperature and are therefore more susceptible to heatstroke. Overweight Aussies have less stamina and endurance because their heart, muscles, and respiratory system are always working overtime—way beyond what they were designed to do. Keep reading—there's more! Overweight Aussies have increased surgical risks, decreased immune functions, and are more susceptible to injuries including damage to joints, bones, and ligaments. Simply put, allowing your Aussie to become overweight subjects him to a diminished quality of life, and he is likely to die at a younger age than his physically fit counterparts.

Is My Australian Shepherd Overweight?

A good, well-balanced diet fed in the proper quantities is the best way to keep your Australian Shepherd fit, lean, and happy, and it can increase his lifespan by nearly 2 years! Generally speaking, most male Aussies weigh between 45 and 60 pounds (20.4 and 27.2 kg), and females between 35 and 45 pounds (15.9 and 20.4 kg). That said, Aussies differ in size, bone structure, and muscularity, so it's impossible to arbitrarily set a correct weight for all Aussies. You can't, for example, say all female Aussies should weigh 45 pounds (20.4 kg), and males 50 pounds (22.7). Some Aussies have really thick coats that can be deceiving. Put your hands on your dog and feel his neck, ribs, and hips.

To be sure your Aussie is not packing extra pounds, follow these simple guidelines for assessing his weight:

- Run your fingers up and down along his ribcage. You should be able to feel the bumps of his ribs without pressing in.
- Run your hand over his croup (his rump). You should be able to feel the bumps of his two pelvic bones with little effort (and without pressing down).

Some owners think if they can feel their Aussie's ribs, he's too thin. Not so! You want your Aussie to be fit and lean. Not too skinny, but not too fat. Ideally, when looking at your Aussie from the side, his abdominal tuck—the underline of his body where his belly appears to draw up toward his hind end—should be evident. When standing over your Aussie and viewing him from above, his waist—the section behind his ribs—should be well proportioned. An overweight Aussie will have a layer of fat covering his ribs, and you will have difficulty feeling them. His abdominal tuck may still be present, but his waist, when viewed from above, will be more difficult, if not impossible, to distinguish. If your Aussie is very overweight or obese—his appearance alone should be a good indicator. You won't be able to feel his ribs because of the heavy layer of fat covering them. He'll probably have fat deposits on his back and hip region, spine, chest, shoulders, neck, and legs. His tummy will hang down, and his belly will probably look distended.

Your veterinarian can help you determine the ideal weight for your Aussie, and develop a long-term plan to condition his body and provide him with a longer, healthier, and happier life.

The Battle of the Bulge

How can you help your Australian Shepherd fight the battle of the bulge? If your Australian Shepherd is currently overweight or obese, the first step should be a trip to the veterinarian. Some medical conditions, such as hypothyroidism and Cushing's disease, can contribute to weight gain, but those cases represent a very small portion of overweight dogs, perhaps less than 5 percent, according to

experts. Some medications, such as prednisone and phenobarbital, can influence a dog's metabolism and appetite. A veterinarian can exam your Aussie to assess his overall health and medical condition, and can advice you on sensible and healthy ways to reduce your Aussie's weight.

If your Australian Shepherd is not overweight, do not allow him to gain extra pounds. Losing weight can be just as tough for dogs as it is for humans and, in the long run, keeping him fit and trim is the kindest thing you can do for him.

Feeding the Right Food

To keep your Australian Shepherd's figure fit and trim, and his muscles lean and hard, choose the food that best suits his activity level and life stage. Overweight and underweight dogs, as well as puppies, athletic, and geriatric dogs have different nutritional and caloric requirements. Puppies require specially formulated diets. An older, less active Australian Shepherd will generally need fewer calories than a young, energetic Aussie, and an overweight Aussie may require a special reduced-calorie diet. When in doubt, always seek veterinary assistance in choosing the food that best suits your Aussie.

Your veterinarian can help you determine the ideal weight for your Aussie.

Table Scraps

If you find yourself sneaking your four-legged friend a tidbit of steak or a French fry or two from the supper table, grow a thick skin and ignore his pleading stares. Table scraps are the worst offenders when it comes to sabotaging your Aussie's weight maintenance program. A tasty tidbit of steak here, a nibble of chicken there, a potato skin, a French fry or

two—what's the harm, right? It is better for table scraps to go to waste than your Aussie's waist. If you cannot resist feeding table scraps, put them in the refrigerator and feed them at a later time as a training treat. Feeding from the table also encourages begging, and Aussies quickly become skilled in the art of begging.

Treats

When choosing treats, read labels carefully and choose treats that are low in fat, sugar, and salt. Small pieces of fruit or fresh veggies are good alternatives to store-bought treats. Or, try baking your four-legged friend some yummy, low-fat, homemade treats. Treats should be a reward for a job well done, such as coming when called. Treats should never be a substitute for well-deserved hugs and kisses.

Exercise!!!

Exercise is ideal for improving your Aussie's overall physical and mental health. It not only helps to burn calories, it strengthens your dog's respiratory system, aids in digestion, and helps get oxygen to tissues. Exercise keeps muscles toned and joints flexible. It releases boredom and keeps your Aussie's mind active. The majority of behavior problems in Aussies, such as digging, chewing, and barking, are a direct result of too little exercise. Equally important, interactive exercise can help strengthen the human–canine bond. And the best part? It's free!

If your Aussie is overweight or out of shape, start slow, and progress at a rate that is within your dog's physical capabilities. Sore muscles and injuries are no fun! If you are uncertain about the amount and method of exercise, always seek veterinary advice. A veterinarian can help you design the exercise program most appropriate for your Aussie's health.

BEGGING

Generally speaking, it is not a good idea to allow your Aussie to beg for food. It's a short leap from sad and pathetic to seasoned beggar! Of course, if you don't mind your 50-pound dog shoving his head in your lap, drooling, pawing, snorting, and staring pathetically while you eat—have at it!

On the other hand, if you prefer your Aussie show some modicum of good manners, you should discourage the behavior of begging from day one. Some owners are under the mistaken impression that treating

their Aussie to tasty tidbits of people food will make him love them more—hence, the old adage about killing your dog with kindness. Aussies who are rewarded for begging quickly learn to manipulate you. And, as mentioned earlier, Aussies are very quick studies in the art of begging.

It really comes down to expectations and management. How you expect your Aussie to behave as he grows and matures into an adult dog. Aussies who do not have boundaries grow into unruly hooligans. If you allow begging…where do you draw the line? What about swiping food off the kitchen counter or, heaven forbid, the supper table? If your Aussie thinks he can get away with begging and stealing food, what about guarding his food bowl or favorite toy? What about growling and snapping at his owners? Once you have decided on your expectations, such as no begging, you manage his environment so that he is not put in a position where he is allowed to develop bad habits.

Puppies should be kept away from the table while you eat, so they are not inadvertently rewarded by dropped food. An alternative is to use a baby gate to keep your dog corralled in another room and away from the table. He will be able to see you while you eat and also get used to waiting patiently without constantly being nagged.

If your Aussie is well trained, you can put him on a *down-stay* while you eat, and then verbally praise him for being a good boy. A word of caution: It is difficult, if not impossible, for most dogs, especially young Aussies, to maintain their composure while in the presence of food. It is better to restrict his access to the dinner table than to continually nag him to stop begging.

Preventing begging behaviors is easy if you make it a rule from day one that no one—this includes kids, spouses, in-laws, and visitors—feeds the dog from the table or at any other time while they are eating.

That said, if your Aussie is already begging, there's a good chance someone has been sneaking him tidbits of food. Aussies are intelligent, and they know a good thing when they see it—or taste it! If you cannot resist sharing your food, put scraps in the refrigerator and feed them at a later time as a training treat. Use the tidbits to teach your Aussie to down, rollover, spin, speak, or sit up and beg properly—as a trick! Remember, any table scraps or bits and pieces of food, even when used as training treats, should be included in your dog's daily caloric count. Otherwise, your Aussie is likely to start packing on extra pounds.

SNAPPING

Some puppies seem to naturally take food nicely without trying to trim your cuticles or chew your fingers. Other puppies must be taught early not to bite the hand that feeds them—literally! It is in your Aussie's best interest for you to nip this behavior in the bud. Left unchecked, it can get downright nasty. Keep in mind, you may inadvertently be teaching your puppy to snatch at food if you are pulling your hand away as he starts to take the food.

If your Aussie has already developed the annoying and painful habit of snapping or snatching food, try this approach: Hold a tasty tidbit of food in the palm of your hand and then fold your hand so you make a fist. Offer him the back of your hand. He will be able to smell the treat, but your fingers will not be exposed or vulnerable. Most likely, he will sniff your hand trying to expose the treat. If he is gentle, open your hand and present the treat in the palm of your hand. He will be able to take the treat without nipping your fingers. As he does so, praise warmly: "Good puppy!" Eventually, he will learn to wait until you have opened your hand before he gets a treat.

Foods to Die For

Dogs have different metabolisms, and some human foods (and non-food items) can cause serious health problems, ranging from a mild upset stomach to death. Your Aussie should not get the final word when it comes to what is and is not good for him. After all, most Aussies will gleefully eat poop, rocks, dirt, and disemboweled squirrels, if left to their own devices. The list below is a sampling of some of the most common foods that can cause your Aussie serious health problems if ingested. It is in your dog's best interest to keep these items from his possession. If you suspect your Aussie has ingested a toxic substance, do not delay. Seek veterinary attention immediately.

- **Alcoholic beverages** can cause intoxication, coma, and, in some instances, death.
- **Bones** from fish, poultry, or other meat sources can cause obstruction or laceration of the digestive system.
- **Cat food**, while not fatal, is high in protein and fat and particularly appetizing for enterprising Aussies. Too much can cause intestinal upset, vomiting, diarrhea, and unnecessary weight gain.
- **Chocolate**—oh, so yummy for people, but deadly for dogs. It can increase a dog's heart rate and breathing, resulting in serious illness and death.
- **Grapes** and **raisins** contain an unknown toxin that can damage your Australian Shepherd's kidneys.
- **Mushrooms** contain toxins that vary depending on the species. They affect multiple systems, resulting in shock and death. They grow in the wild—and your backyard. Closely supervise your dog to prevent ingestion.
- **Onions** and **garlic** contain sulfoxides and disulfides, which can be toxic to dogs, damaging red blood cells and causing anemia.
- **Tobacco** contains nicotine and can cause an increased heartbeat, collapse, coma, and death.

DOGGY DIETS: A COMPARISON

CANNED FOOD

Advantages

- High palatability
- Easier to digest
- Contains a higher meat protein level
- Canning process kills harmful bacteria
- Long shelf life

Disadvantages

- More expensive than dry foods
- Provides no abrasion from chewing, which allows faster plaque and tartar build-up on teeth
- Requires refrigeration after opening
- High-heat processing can destroy some nutrients
- Due to high water content, moist foods have fewer nutrients than other foods.
- More food must be eaten to satisfy energy and nutrient needs

DRY FOOD

Advantages

- Economical, readily available, and convenient to buy, store, and use
- Good shelf life; does not require refrigeration
- May improve dental hygiene through chewing and grinding, which aids in the removal of dental plaque, although this is highly debatable among the experts (does not eliminate the need for regular dental care)
- Provides some exercise for a dog's mouth, and helps satisfy a puppy's need to chew
- High-quality brands have high caloric density and good digestibility, which means lower amounts per serving must be consumed
- Stool is usually smaller and more compact

Disadvantages

- Less palatable to some dogs than canned or semi-moist foods
- High heat used in the processing stage can destroy valuable nutrients

SEMI-MOIST FOOD

Advantages

- High sugar content may increase palatability
- Less offensive smelling than canned foods
- Good shelf life. Does not require refrigeration

Disadvantages

- High sugar levels in dog food can cause spikes in blood sugar levels and contribute to obesity
- High sugar levels may aggravate an existing or borderline diabetic condition
- Contains high levels of salt
- Contains propylene glycol
- Sticky, sugary foods can contribute to dental disease
- If left out for long periods, such as in a dog bowl, it will dry out, reducing palatability

BONES AND RAW FOOD DIET (BARF)

Advantages

- You control the ingredients
- Proponents believe dogs live longer, have healthy lives, and better immune systems

Disadvantages

- Time-consuming to prepare
- Difficult to find fresh, high-quality raw meats
- More expensive, especially if using organic foods
- Difficult to achieve complete and balanced levels of nutrients on a regular basis
- Concern of bacterial infections, parasites, and food-borne illnesses for both dogs and humans when handling and eating raw foods (i.e., *E. coli* and *Salmonella*)
- Choking hazards when eating raw bones

HOMEMADE FOOD

Advantages

- You control the ingredients
- You can customize by providing a mixture of fresh meat, chicken, fish, vegetables, and commercial kibble
- You can provide a combination of cooked and raw ingredients

Disadvantages

- Time-consuming to prepare
- More expensive, especially if using organic ingredients
- Difficult to achieve complete and balanced levels of nutrients on a regular basis
- Concern of bacterial infections, parasites, and food-borne illnesses for both dogs and humans handling and eating raw foods (i.e., *E. coli* and *Salmonella*)

5

GROOMING

Your Australian Shepherd

The Australian Shepherd is a double-coated breed with a moderate length topcoat (or outer coat), and a soft, downy undercoat that develops as the dog reaches adulthood. For the companion Aussie, as opposed to the show dog, grooming is a relatively easy process as long as it is done with regularity and your dog views it as a positive and enjoyable experience.

Grooming your Aussie on a regular basis keeps his skin and coat in tip-top condition, and allows you to check his entire body for lumps, bumps, cuts, rashes, dry skin, fleas, ticks, stickers, and the like. You can check his feet for cuts, torn pads or broken nails, and examine his mouth for signs of trouble including tartar, broken teeth, or discolored gums. Most Aussies love to be groomed, making this necessary chore a great way to spend quality time with your dog while simultaneously building a strong and mutually trusting human–canine relationship. Equally important, when you regularly groom your Aussie, you will quickly recognize when something is amiss.

It's also a good idea to start instilling good grooming practices right away. If your puppy came from a reputable breeder, he is probably used to being handled and gently stroked. He's probably had at least one bath and may already be accustomed to and tolerate being brushed and examined. A puppy who is exposed to positive and delightful grooming experiences will grow into an adult dog who takes pleasure in the regular routine. Few things are as frustrating as trying to wrestle down a 50-pound Australian Shepherd who hates to be groomed.

ACCEPTING GROOMING

Don't despair if grooming is new to your Aussie. Like anything else, it is best to start slow and progress at a rate that is suitable for the age and mental maturity of your dog.

If you have a grooming table, begin by teaching your Aussie to stand on the table. For a puppy, any sturdy surface such as a bench or crate top covered with a non-skid, non-slip surface is sufficient. Sitting or kneeling on the floor with your Aussie works too. In addition to standing, teach your Aussie to lie down and relax on the table. This position is helpful when trimming his nails, brushing his tummy, and examining his body for stickers, burs, cuts, hot spots, and such. Aussies who learn to relax on a grooming table are more likely to relax on a veterinarian's examination table, making a trip to the vet's office less stressful for all involved.

Have all the grooming tools out and within easy reach *before* you start grooming. Never turn your back or leave your Aussie on a grooming table unattended. It takes only a second for a young Aussie to injure himself should he fall or jump.

Puppies have limited attention spans, so do not expect your Aussie to remain still for extended periods of time. In the beginning, you want progress—not perfection. Your goal is for him to stand or lie still for a few seconds while you praise him. Harsh handling during these learning stages will come back to haunt you when your Aussie begins resenting this necessary chore. Progress to the point where your puppy will accept having his body stroked with your hand, then gently, slowly, and calmly brush him all over. In the beginning, your Aussie may be frightened, nervous, or unsure. Patience, gentle handling, and plenty of hugs and kisses will help to build his confidence and teach him to accept and enjoy the grooming process.

THE GROOMING TABLE

Aussies are pretty agile, and jumping on and off a grooming table can be a fun game for them. But they run the risk of injuring themselves—especially if they are jumping onto hard or slippery concrete. An adult Aussie may be too heavy for some people to lift, but don't discard the grooming table! Teach him "feet up"—which is to put his front feet on the grooming table, then you boost his back legs up and onto the table. (This works great for boosting dogs into SUVs, vans, and larger cars.) Most dogs learn "feet up" when owners pat the table and say the command "feet up." When the dog puts his feet up—praise and reward. If he doesn't get the hang of "feet up," simply lift his front feet onto the table, then hoist his rear legs up.

Getting off the table is a bit trickier. Most owners employ a lifting and jumping combination. Put one of your arms between your dog's front legs, and your other arm wrapped under his chest/stomach area. As the dog jumps, your arm positioning helps guide him and cushion a hard landing. You certainly don't want him jumping off the table by himself onto concrete and hurting himself. Some companies manufacture ramps specifically for loading dogs in and out of cars, onto grooming tables,

Stripping

You "strip" a dog when the undercoat has died. A stripping comb will help pull out the dead hairs from the undercoat, which allows the new undercoat to grow in more quickly. It can take several stripping sessions to remove all of the undercoat. If possible, do this outdoors because it creates quite a mess.

and other hard-to-reach places. If you are handy with a hammer and nails, you can make your own or build a couple of stackable boxes on which he can climb up and down.

COAT AND SKIN CARE

The Aussie does not have high-maintenance grooming needs, but you will have to take some time to care for his skin and coat. The tools you'll need include:

Brushing
- Pin brush
- Slicker brush
- Stripping comb
- Steel comb
- Spray bottle

Bathing
- Shampoo and conditioner made specifically for dogs
- Towels
- Blow dryer (optional)

Grooming tables are a necessity for show dogs.

Brushing

For most Aussies, a pin brush for long hair, a slicker brush with bent wire teeth for removing mats and shedding hair, a stripping comb for removing undercoat, and a steel comb with teeth divided between fine and coarse for removing debris, are sufficient for day-to-day grooming and whisking away pieces of debris, dust, dirt, and dead hair. Regular brushings are essential for removing dead hairs, promoting and distributing natural oils, and bringing out the shine and natural luster in an Aussie's coat. Regular brushings also prevent the undercoat from matting.

An Australian Shepherd's double coat means they shed—and they can shed a lot. The amount of shedding, which is a natural process in which strands of hair die, fall out (shed), and are replaced by new hairs, varies according to the dog, the season, and climatic conditions. Most Aussies shed heavily in the spring or early summer when they tend to "blow coat."

When properly cared for on a regular basis, an Aussie's coat is relatively easy to maintain. Like anything else, however, if neglected,

Anal Glands

Dogs have anal glands on each side of the anus. When viewing a dog from behind, they are located at approximately the four and eight o'clock positions. The glands are emptied naturally with bowel movements. However, it is not uncommon for them to become impacted (clogged), infected, or abscessed. When the glands become full and uncomfortable, an Aussie may scoot along the floor, or lick the anal area excessively. Abscessed or infected glands can be very painful, and a dog may be hesitant to allow you to touch the area.

When glands become clogged, they must be expressed, or emptied, by applying pressure to the glands. While some owners have learned to express the glands themselves, most prefer to leave it to a veterinarian. Abscessed anal glands require veterinary attention, as do some impacted or clogged glands.

it can take the better part of a year to restore it to a good and healthy condition.

Shaving Aussies is a controversial topic. Many owners do it in the summer to keep their Aussie cool. Others do it to reduce the necessary chore of regular brushings or to remove deeply embedded mats. However, shaving an Aussie's coat leaves him vulnerable to sunburn—especially merle-colored dogs—and removes his natural protection from stickers and burs.

How to Brush Your Australian Shepherd

Brushing a dry coat can cause hair breakage and damage. Therefore, throughout the brushing process, regularly mist or spray your Aussie's hair with a coat dressing, coat conditioner diluted with water, or plain water. This protects the hair and controls static as you brush.

Most breeders and groomers recommend starting at the dog's head—brushing the top of the head and around the ears, down the neck, chest, and front legs. Then brush in one long stroke from the head toward the tail; brush down the sides, and finish with the rear legs. Most discourage backward brushing—brushing against the direction of hair growth—because it can damage the coat, and some dogs find the process uncomfortable and annoying. Be sure to brush down to the skin, brushing both the top coat and undercoat. Brushing only the top coat can result in painful mats and tangles that are difficult, if not impossible, to comb out. When a matted coat gets wet, the moisture is trapped near the skin, causing hot spots—circular lesions that are inflamed, raw, moist, and very painful.

Many Aussies, especially males, can have quite a lot of feathering on their legs—the hair that runs from the elbow to the pastern (or wrist) area. Everything from dirt to mud to snowballs to freshly mowed lawn clippings accumulate in leg featherings. Keeping this area cleaned and brushed is important to prevent painful mats and coat damage. If you have no plans to show your Aussie, consider trimming the feathering short for convenience sake. It can save you a lot of time and energy, especially during wet or snowy weather.

Pay attention to the soft fuzzy hair behind the ears, too. It mats easily, so it needs to be kept clean and brushed regularly. Thinning the fuzzy hair will help to prevent matting while keeping your Aussie's coat tidy. Remember, your Aussie's skin is sensitive, despite his brawn! Brush gently; don't tug or pull, because this can hurt. Part the hair with one hand and work from the skin out with the brush. Be careful

Keep a towel handy to dry off your Aussie.

not to brush the skin itself with a slicker brush, because this can create nicks, scratches, and even welts—often referred to as *slicker burn*.

Once-a-week brushings are usually sufficient, but a 5-minute once-a-day once over with a pin or slicker brush is ideal to keep your Aussie's coat glossy and gorgeous, and keep shedding to a minimum.

Finish the coat and add shine by applying a small amount of specially designed coat dressing or coat oil. This protects the coat from the elements and helps to prevent burs and debris from sticking to the coat.

Bathing

How often your Aussie requires bathing depends on where you live, how much time he spends outside, and how dirty he gets. Like kids, some Aussies have a knack for getting dirtier than others. A working dog may require bathing on a regular basis, say, every 4 to 6 weeks or so. Aussies who spend a great deal of time indoors may require bathing once every 3 or 4 months. No cut-and-dried formula is applied; you be the judge.

Most Aussies enjoy the water and are quite amenable to baths. In hot climates, you may be able to bathe your dog outdoors with a garden hose, provided the water is not too cold. Otherwise, a rubber mat on the bottom of a bathtub or shower stall will provide secure footing and prevent him from slipping. Don't forget slippery floors,

Invest in Good Equipment

If you plan to groom your Australian Shepherd—as opposed to having him professionally groomed—invest in good, professional-quality equipment. The initial investment will cost a bit more, but in the long run you won't be replacing brushes and combs every few months. When properly cared for, good quality grooming tools will last a lifetime.

Start at the head when brushing.

either. A rubber mat or plenty of dry towels on the bathroom floor will prevent your Aussie from slipping and injuring himself as he jumps out of the tub. Consider also investing in a grooming apron—or a raincoat! Aussies love two things: shaking when they are wet, and rubbing their wet bodies against your legs or any other nearby surface including walls, floors, and furniture. So have plenty of towels on hand for cleaning up and drying off. Invest in a screen that fits over the drain opening, which helps keep your dog's excess hair from clogging your drains.

Unless your dog has a specific skin condition, such as dry, flaky, itchy skin, choose a good quality shampoo and conditioner designed specifically for dogs—something non-toxic and shampoo-based, rather than detergent-based so as not to strip the hair of its natural oils. Many shampoos and conditioning products are available, from all-purpose to medicating to herbal to color enhancing, so do not be shy about asking for help when choosing shampoos and conditioners.

How to Bathe Your Australian Shepherd

Saturate your Aussie's coat, undercoat, and skin with warm water. This can take some time if your Aussie has a thick coat. Apply a dab or two of shampoo and scrub away! Work the shampoo into the coat with your fingers or a rubber massage tool designed specifically for dogs. Scrub from head to toe, being careful to avoid the eye area. Don't overlook his belly, the inside of his hind legs, under his arms, and behind his ears. To clean around an Aussie's eyes, wipe the area with a damp cloth. You can use a small dab of tearless shampoo to gently wash around the head and eye area. Even though it is tearless, avoid getting any in your dog's eyes. Rinse his entire body thoroughly with tepid or lukewarm water until the water runs clear. Rinsing is the most important part because an Aussie's coat can hold a lot of suds, and residual shampoo can irritate the skin, as well as leave a dull film on the coat. If necessary, shampoo and rinse again to be sure your Aussie is squeaky clean. If you are using a coat conditioner or skin moisturizer, follow the directions carefully.

If possible, let your Aussie shake off any extra water, then towel dry him thoroughly.

Take care to protect him from any drafts or getting chilled. This is especially important for young puppies, aging Aussies, and pregnant bitches. If you live where temperatures are warm, and your Aussie is likely to air dry quickly, blow-drying is usually not necessary. If you choose to complete the process by blow-drying, hold the dryer at least 6 inches away from the coat, keep the dryer in motion, and use a low or cool setting to avoid damaging the coat or burning your dog's skin.

A word of caution: Wet Aussies love to roll in whatever is handy, be it grass, dirt, mud, or gravel. Consider keeping him sequestered until he is dry. Otherwise, before you can say *squeaky clean*, he will happily undo all your hard work!

DENTAL CARE

Just as you take good care of your teeth, it is essential that you take good care of your Aussie's teeth. The importance of high-quality dental hygiene cannot be overstated. If left unattended, your Aussie can develop periodontal disease, a progressive disease that can, in advanced cases, lead to decayed gums, infection, and liver, kidney, and heart damage. It is estimated that 80 percent of dogs over the age of 3 years have some stage of periodontal disease. And, like humans, dogs experience painful toothaches, although some dogs—especially Australian Shepherds who tend to be very stoic—may not physically exhibit signs of pain, or the signs may be subtle and overlooked by some owners.

Plaque and Tartar

Dental problems in dogs begin the same way they do in humans—with plaque. Plaque is a mixture of salivary glycoproteins—a colorless, translucent adhesive fluid—and it is the major culprit in periodontal disease. Plaque begins with an accumulation of food particles and bacteria along the gumline. Germs present in plaque attack the gums, bone, and ligaments that support the teeth. Routine home care can help to remove this plaque. However, when left untreated, minerals and saliva combine with the plaque and harden into a substance called *tartar*, or calculus. As tartar accumulates, it starts irritating your dog's gums, causing an inflamed condition called *gingivitis*, which is easily identified by the yellowish-brown crust on the teeth and the reddening

Grooming as a Health Check

An Australian Shepherd's coat is a mirror reflection of his health. As you brush, pay particular attention to the condition of his coat. Check to see:

- Is your Australian Shepherd's coat healthy and shiny? Or is it dull, brittle, and lackluster?

- Is his skin dry and flaky?

- Does it have a bad smell or that unmistakable doggie odor?

- Do you see bare spots where hair is missing?

Any of these conditions could be a sign of inadequate grooming, internal illness, parasite infestation, or an inadequate diet. When in doubt, a veterinarian can diagnosis the problem and recommended suitable treatments.

Dog Tooth Structure

Experts often compare the structure of a dog's tooth to that of an iceberg. What you see above the surface is the tip of the tooth—or the "tip of the iceberg." The portion of the tooth that lies below the gum's surface is much larger, and it is easy to ignore what you cannot see. Unfortunately, by the time you notice tartar on the surface of your dog's teeth, you can be certain damage below the surface of the gums is well under way.

of gums next to the teeth.

In the early stages, periodontal disease, which results from the buildup of plaque and tartar around and under the gumline, is generally reversible provided your Aussie receives veterinary attention along with sufficient and regular brushings at home. Otherwise, the process continues to erode the tissues and bones that support the teeth, which can lead to pain and tooth loss. As bad as that sounds, it can get worse.

If the tartar is not removed, the cycle continues to repeat itself, encouraging even more bacterial growth. The tartar builds up under the gums and causes the gums to separate from the teeth; this causes even larger pockets in which more debris can collect. At this stage, it's likely your Aussie's teeth have quite an accumulation of highly visible crusty yellowish-brown tartar. Brushing your Aussie's teeth on a regular basis will remove plaque but not tartar. If your Aussie already has a tartar buildup, he needs to see a veterinarian to have it removed and his teeth inspected, cleaned, and polished.

In most advanced stages, damage from periodontal disease is considered irreversible because bacterial infection has been busy destroying your Aussie's gums, teeth, and bones. Treatment, which can include difficult and extensive surgeries, will not reverse the damage, but it will help to prevent further progression, additional pain and discomfort to your Aussie, and guard against bacteria entering the bloodstream to cause secondary infections that can damage your dog's heart, liver, and kidneys.

Annual Exams

In addition to home-care, a good dental hygiene program includes an annual veterinary examination. A veterinarian will check for potential problems, such as plaque and tartar build-up, gingivitis, periodontal disease, and fractured or abscessed teeth. If necessary, a veterinarian may recommend professional dental cleaning, also known as prophylaxis or prophy. While anesthetized, a dog's mouth is flushed with a solution to kill bacteria; the teeth are cleaned to remove any tartar, polished, inspected, and flushed again with an antibacterial solution; and fluoride is applied. In most cases, x-rays will also be taken. Fractured teeth may require reconstructive surgery not unlike people receive, such as root canals and crowns.

The best way to prevent periodontal disease is to keep your Aussie's teeth clean. The process is relatively simple and requires nothing more than a small number of fairly inexpensive supplies and a few minutes of your time.

How to Brush Your Australian Shepherd's Teeth

You will need:

- A pet toothbrush, gauze for wrapping around a finger, or a finger toothbrush
- Toothpaste designed specifically for dogs.

A finger brush, as the name suggests, simply slides over your finger. If you go with a pet toothbrush, be sure to get one specially designed for an Australian Shepherd or the mouth of a medium-breed dog. A small toothbrush designed for, say, a Pug, will do little for your Australian Shepherd. A word of caution: Do not use human toothpaste. It can upset your dog's stomach. Most canine toothpastes are formulated with poultry or malt flavored enhancers for easier acceptance.

As with other aspects of grooming, it is much easier to begin introducing oral hygiene to a puppy, but it is never too late to begin—just start slowly and progress at a pace suitable for your Aussie. Most dogs, be they young or old, will take issue with a toothbrush being jammed in their mouth, so start by using your finger to gently massage his gums. Put a small dab of doggie toothpaste on your index finger, and let your dog lick it. Praise him for being brave! Apply another dab on your finger, gently lift up his outer lips, and massage his gums.

Ideally, it is best to massage in a circular motion but, in the beginning, you may need to be satisfied with simply getting your finger in your dog's mouth. Try to massage both top and bottom, and the front gums, too. Watch out for those sharp baby teeth, and remember to keep a positive attitude, praising and reassuring your Aussie throughout the process. It is also helpful if you try to avoid wrestling with your dog or restraining him too tightly. This will only hamper the process and make him resistant to the necessary routine.

Depending on your dog, it may take a few days or a few weeks for him to accept you fiddling about in his mouth. With any luck, he will eventually come to look forward to the routine. That is the long-term goal. It is possible he may never come to enjoy it, but it is important that he learns to accept it.

Once your dog is comfortable with this process, try using a toothbrush, finger toothbrush, or a gauze pad wrapped around your

Four Types of Teeth

Dogs have four types of teeth and each has a different function:

- Incisors are used for cutting and nibbling food.
- Canines are used for holding and tearing food.
- Premolars are used for cutting, holding, and shearing food.
- Molars are for grinding food.

Ideally, you should brush your Aussie's teeth on a daily basis, just as you do your own teeth. Like anything else, the hardest part is getting started. However, once you accustom your Aussie to having his teeth brushed, incorporating the practice into your daily schedule is no more difficult or time consuming than brushing your own teeth.

finger. Let your dog lick some toothpaste off the toothbrush or gauze pad and, again, praise him for being brave! This will help accustom him to the texture of the brush or gauze while building his confidence.

You are now ready to begin brushing. As before, lift the outer lips and expose the teeth. Most owners find it easiest to start with the canine teeth—the large ones in the front of the mouth. They are the easiest to reach, and you should be able to brush them with little interference or objection from your dog. Once your dog is accustomed to you brushing a few teeth, progress to a few more, then a few more until you have brushed all 42 teeth (or 28 teeth if you have a puppy).

Chews and Food for Dental Hygiene

You can try using any number of chew or dental toys available for dogs that help to remove plaque. Select products that are right for the chewing style of your Australian Shepherd, and that are made to last. Toys should not replace brushing, but they will help to remove some of the plaque, exercise your Aussie's jaw, and satisfy his need to chew. Keep an eye on these toys, and toss them when they get too small and become possible choking hazards. Avoid toys and bones that are hard enough to crack or break an aggressive chewer's teeth. Nylabone makes toys that are suitable for an Aussie.

Many veterinarians recommend avoiding table scraps and sweet treats, because they can increase the buildup of plaque. A high-quality, crunchy dog food may help to keep plaque from accumulating on teeth; however, this topic is highly debatable among the experts. Either way, a dry, crunchy food is definitely better for exercising your dog's jaw. Veterinary dentist-approved dog food is available that is designed to help reduce plaque and tartar buildup. Your veterinarian can provide information on these products.

EAR CARE

An Australian Shepherd's ear canal is warm, dark, and moist, making it an ideal site for bacterial or yeast infections, tumors, and parasites, such as ear mites. Unlike a human's ear canal, which lies basically in a horizontal line from the side of the head inward to the eardrum, a dog's ear canal is L-shaped. The internal ear canal descends vertically before making a roughly 45-degree bend and terminating in a horizontal stretch to the eardrum—also known as the *tympanic membrane*. Debris loves to collect in the 45-degree bend of the ear canal.

The key to preventing ear problems is to keep ears clean, and to know the difference between a clean-smelling ear and a problem ear. A healthy ear should have a clean, healthy doggy smell—resembling the smell of beeswax, somewhat. Honey-colored wax in the ear is normal, but a crusty, dark substance may indicate problems, such as ear mites. An infected ear has an unmistakably foul odor. Ear infections are serious, and should never be ignored or taken lightly. If your Aussie's ears have a discharge; smell bad; the canals look abnormal, red, or inflamed; or your dog is showing signs of discomfort, such as depression or irritability, scratching or rubbing his ears or head, shaking his head or tilting it to one side—these are signs of a problem. Seek veterinary attention right away. An ear infection left untreated can cause permanent damage to a dog's hearing.

To help prevent problems, get in the habit of examining your Aussie's ears regularly for wax, ear mites, and other irritations. If your Aussie walks or plays in pastures, fields, or areas with heavy underbrush—check his ears frequently for stickers, burs, and other foreign matters.

How to Clean Your Australian Shepherd's Ears

You'll need:

- An ear-cleaning product specifically designed for dogs
- Cotton or gauze pad

Place a few drops of cleaner into the dog's ear canal and gently massage the base of the ear for about 20 seconds. This helps to soften and loosen the debris. When you're done, let your dog have a good head shake to eject the cleaning solution and debris from the ear canal. Next, apply some ear-cleaning solution onto a clean cotton or gauze pad. Gently wipe the inside ear leather (ear flap), and the part of the ear canal that you can see.

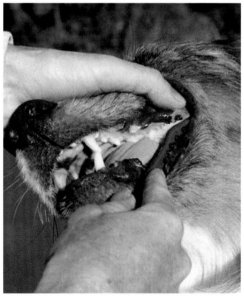

Remember the old adage, "Never stick anything smaller than your elbow in your ear"? The same concept applies to dogs. Never stick cotton applicator swaps or pointed objects into the ear canal because this tends to pack the debris rather than remove it. More important, you risk injuring your dog's eardrum should you probe too deeply.

If you suspect problems, seek veterinary attention right away and leave the probing to the experts.

To avoid periodontal disease, you must keep your Aussie's teeth and gums healthy.

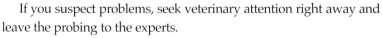

NAIL CARE

Nail trimming is a necessary part of dog ownership. Few Aussies, especially those who spend the majority of their time indoors or on grass when outdoors, will wear down their nails naturally. If your dog makes an unmistakable *click, click, click* as he walks on hard floors—his nails are too long. Ideally, a dog's nails should not touch the ground. This allows a dog to stand squarely and compactly on the pads of his feet. Nails that are too long interfere with a dog's gait—making walking awkward or painful. Equally important, long nails can be broken, torn off, or snagged, and can scratch furniture, hardwood floors, and skin. Torn or broken nails can cause an Aussie a great deal of pain and discomfort, and they may become infected, which can require veterinary attention to remove the nail completely.

As with other aspects of grooming, introduce your Aussie to the practice of nail care at a young age. With any luck, the breeder will have started nail clipping as part of the socialization process, as well as to build the puppy's confidence and teach him to accept having his feet handled.

If you choose to clip the nails yourself, invest in a good-quality nail clipper designed specifically for dogs. In the beginning, depending on the puppy's level of cooperation, you may want to simply touch the nail clipper to the puppy's nail and then offer plenty of praise. Then progress to clipping tiny bits of nail and then trimming off the remaining dead nail in small bits.

In the early stages, you may need someone to help hold your dog, but once you get used to it, trimming your Aussie's nails is no more difficult than trimming your own. When in doubt, ask a veterinarian, groomer, or breeder to show you how to do it properly. Or have a professional trim them regularly, which can mean once a week or once a month—or somewhere in between—depending on the dog.

How to Cut Your Australian Shepherd's Nails

You'll need:
- A high-quality nail clipper designed for dogs
- Styptic powder or pencil

Owners are often reluctant to trim their dogs' nails for fear of hurting the dog or making him bleed. Dogs have a blood vessel that travels approximately three-quarters of the way through the nail. This is called the "quick." Clipping a dog's nails too short can cut the quick and cause bleeding. However, learning how to do it properly,

Doggie Bad Breath

Also known as *halitosis*, bad breath generally indicates something more serious, such as periodontal disease, diabetes, kidney disease, or gastrointestinal problems. Unless you have seen your Aussie eat something particularly offensive like spoiled garbage, squirrel guts, cat stools, another dog's stools, or even his own stools—yes, some dogs find this appetizing—it is best to have your dog examined by a veterinarian. If left untreated, some causes of bad breath can cause severe and even fatal complications.

using the correct equipment, and having a dog who accepts having his feet handled, will go a long way in reducing the odds of inadvertently nipping the quick.

Your Aussie may have white or black nails or a combination. Black nails can make it difficult to differentiate between the quick and the hook—the dead section of nail that extends beyond the quick.

Examine the underside of the nail before clipping. The section closest to the paw is solid, while the tip—or hook—of the nail looks hollow, like a shell. You may be able to see or feel the slightest groove on the underside hook portion of the nail. Trim only the portion between the solid nail and the thinner hollow part—just tipping it where it curves slightly downward.

One of the easiest ways to trim the nails on the front feet is to have the dog sitting. Lift and hold one foot about 6 inches or so off the ground, so you can see the nail clearly, then trim away. With young or inexperienced dogs, you may have to put the foot back down between nails. Much will depend on the how cooperative the dog is. With the rear nails, it is easier to have the dog standing. Lift the foot off the ground about 4 to 6 inches, and trim away. Some people find it easier to lift the rear foot and extend the leg backwards, not unlike the position a horse's leg is in when you are working on his feet. Some people have their dog lie on the floor—this works in a pinch, too. It is really a matter of preference, what is easiest for you, and what the dog will and will not tolerate.

One of the easiest ways to trim the nails on the front feet is to have the dog sitting.

Dewclaws

If your Australian Shepherd has dewclaws, be sure not to overlook them in the trimming process. Dewclaws are the fifth digit on the inside of the front legs, usually an inch or so above the feet. If left unattended, they can curl around and grow into the soft tissue, not unlike an ingrown toenail on a human. Some breeders have the dewclaws removed, so your Aussie may or may not have them.

C h a p t e r

6

TRAINING AND BEHAVIOR
of Your Australian Shepherd

One of the great pleasures of owning an Australian Shepherd is training him. Aussies are quick to learn, eager to please, and, on most occasions, a bit too clever for their own good. This can make training them simultaneously exhilarating and exhausting for experienced and novice owners a like. However, most of the problems you will encounter are entirely predictable. Remember the history and origin of the Aussie breed? They are high-drive, high-energy herding dogs with a propensity for attacking moving objects, herding cats and horses, and chasing fleeing kids on bicycles. By understanding what makes your Aussie tick—why he does what he does—you can head off many of the problems associated with owning a high-drive dog. At the very least, you can prevent them from escalating into major stumbling blocks.

WHY DOGS DO WHAT THEY DO

Understanding how dogs learn greatly increases your chance of success and helps expedite the training process. Canine genetics and animal behavior are complicated and exhausting topics, well beyond the scope of this book. The good news is you do not need a Ph.D. in genetics or animal behavior to figure out what makes your Australian Shepherd tick. Without delving too deeply into the complexities of canine genetics, it is safe to say that dogs do what they do for two reasons: inherited behaviors and acquired behaviors.

Inherited Behaviors

Inherited behaviors—also known as genetic predispositions—are the traits that Mother Nature genetically programmed. These traits are likely to show up at some time in your Aussie's life whether you want them to or not. For example, Australian Shepherds were originally bred as herding dogs, and the instinct to herd is in their genes. This inherent tendency to herd is part and parcel of your puppy's complete package. As a result, most Aussies are high-energy dogs, and more than a few take great pleasure in herding your kids, other animals, and even the vacuum cleaner.

By recognizing and understanding specific predispositions, you can learn to work within

You can learn a lot from your dog's body language— this "play bow" means your Aussie is ready to have some fun!

You can learn a lot from your dog's body language— this "play bow" means your Aussie is ready to have some fun!

the confines of the breed—what the dog has and what he is built to do. You can learn to develop a particular style of handling that gets the best from your particular dog, and you can design a training program that best suits your puppy's individual and inherited characteristics.

Acquired Behaviors

Acquired characteristics are behaviors your puppy has acquired from the day he was born. These behaviors are learned—be they good or bad, desired or undesired. Swiping food off the counter, refusing to come when called, peeing from one end of the house to the other, bolting out the front door, and committing heinous crimes against your personal property are all acquired behaviors. An 8-week-old Australian Shepherd who learns to have fun chasing young children and nipping their pant legs will see no harm in doing this as a 50-pound (22.7 kg) adult dog. An adorable puppy who is mollycoddled every time he whines or barks will grow into an adult Aussie who barks and whines whenever he wants attention. These are acquired behaviors—behaviors that a dog has acquired through learned experiences.

Acquired behaviors can also be positive. If you call your 6-month-old Australian Shepherd, and he comes tearing over to you with his head and ears up, his tail wagging, and a happy attitude that screams, "Here I am!"—that too is an acquired behavior. The dog has learned to happily and eagerly come when called. Dogs who do not beg or steal food, bolt out doors, or refuse to come when called have learned to respect their owners.

SOCIALIZATION

Certain periods in a puppy's life are critical to his social development. What happens within these individual stages has an enormous and significant impact on his future behavior as an adult. Research has shown that puppies are capable of learning at an early age, and they form lasting impressions during these critical periods. These impressions are remembered throughout a dog's life, be they good or bad.

A puppy who is exposed to positive experiences during the socialization period, such as handling, grooming, and different sights and sounds, stands a better chance of developing the socialization skills and coping mechanisms necessary to grow into a mentally sound and confident adult dog. Older puppies who have not been adequately or properly socialized during these periods tend to be more cautious. They generally grow up shy, fearful, and frequently nervous. As an adult dog, they find it difficult, if not impossible, to cope with new experiences. They rarely, if ever, reach their full potential or live their lives to the fullest. This is a disastrous situation for Australian Shepherds.

Socialization is the single most important process in an Aussie's life. Breeders and owners owe it to their puppies to take advantage of these critical periods to maximize their future, foster their zany

Seven Tips for Successful Dog Training

- Puppies and young dogs have limited attention spans. Keep sessions short: train two or three times a day, 5 or 10 minutes per session.
- Training must always be fun. Fun games maximize your dog's propensity to learn.
- Train when your dog is awake and eager to play. Never wake up your dog to train him.
- Dogs learn at different rates. Train within your dog's mental and physical capabilities. Never progress at a speed faster than your dog's ability to comprehend.
- Set achievable goals to keep you and your puppy motivated. Keep training steps small, and praise your dog every time he does a tiny step right.
- Always use a command when you use your dog's name. "Fido, come!" or "Fido, down." If you repeatedly say your dog's name without putting a command with it, it is a form of nagging and eventually your dog will become desensitized to his name.
- Always end a play/training session on a positive note.

Puppies need to be exposed to a variety of sights and smells in a safe and stress-free environment.

personalities, and instill desired behaviors. How much time and energy you invest during this critical period directly impacts the future character of your puppy.

Early Socialization

By the time your puppy is ready to begin his new life at your home, usually between 7 and 8 weeks of age, the process of socialization will have already begun. The breeder will have seen your puppy through the neonatal and transitional periods and halfway through the critical socialization period. During this time, responsible and knowledgeable breeders will ensure their litters are handled daily to accustom them to human contact and imprint trust, which is essential when it comes to raising a sound Australian Shepherd. They may have a radio or television playing to accustom them to different voices and sounds. They make sure the puppies receive individual attention and are exposed to a variety of sights and smells in a safe and stress-free environment. Many breeders will have accustomed their young puppies to crates, thereby facilitating the crate-training process.

For this reason, you must make careful choices about where you acquire your Australian Shepherd. How your puppy is managed during the neonatal, transitional, and socialization periods has a tremendous impact on how he reacts and interacts to various situations and people as an adult dog.

Your Role

Your job begins the day your puppy arrives at your home. There is much to accomplish within a very small window of opportunity, so maximize your time and use it wisely. Your Aussie must learn important socialization skills between 8 and 16 weeks of age. Once this small window of opportunity has passed, it can never be recaptured. Squandering your opportunities during this critical time means your puppy will suffer in the long run. You run the risk of having your Australian Shepherd develop bad habits and associations that are difficult, if not impossible, to correct later in life.

As the owner of a new Aussie puppy, you are assuming the role of parent and pack leader. You are assuming an enormous responsibility that includes protecting him from bad or traumatic experiences, while simultaneously instilling desired behaviors, fostering his upbeat personality, and providing him with every opportunity to grow into a well-adjusted, mentally confident adult dog.

The importance of maximizing your opportunities during this critical period cannot be overly stressed. Puppies mature faster than humans. On the average, humans take about 18 years to reach maturity, while puppies take about 1 to 1.5 years—depending on the dog. Your 8-week-old Aussie will be 8 weeks old for exactly 7 days. The same goes for being 9, 10, 11, and 12 weeks old. While 1 week may seem insignificant in the lifespan of a child, it represents a significant portion of your Aussie's puppyhood. Once those 7 days have passed, they can never be recaptured.

Therefore, if possible, avoid scheduling vacations or extended trips out of town while your puppy is between 8 and 16 weeks of age—unless, of course, you plan to take him with you. Boarding him in a kennel or leaving him in the care of friends or relatives during this time puts your puppy at a serious disadvantage later in life. You will have missed a prime opportunity to shape his future character and instill all the behaviors you want your puppy to possess as an adult dog.

How to Socialize Your Australian Shepherd

Before taking your puppy outdoors and around other animals, consult with your veterinarian about any necessary puppy vaccinations to ensure your Aussie is protected from diseases. Then, in a fun, safe, and stress-free environment, begin exposing your Aussie to a wide variety of people including babies in strollers, toddlers, teenagers, women in floppy hats, and men with power tools. Expose him to other animals in the household, the clapping of hands, the jingling of keys, and the clatter of dog bowls. Let him explore a variety of surfaces including grass, cement, gravel, tile, carpet, linoleum, sand, and dirt. Many dogs— especially herding dogs—are attracted to moving objects, which incite their chase instinct. Your Aussie should be exposed to these

Socialization Tip

If you are interested in showing your Aussie, expose him in a controlled atmosphere to the sights, scents, and sounds that he will encounter later in competition, such as big dogs, small dogs, noisy dogs, vendor booths, blow dryers, crates, baby gates, grooming tables, agility or obedience equipment, sheep, cows, corrals, and so forth.

objects, including strollers, wheelchairs, shopping carts, vacuums, bicycles, and kids on roller skates and skateboards. A puppy who is not exposed to moving objects may be fearful of them, and may try to attack them as he gets older.

He should be exposed to stairways, paper bags blowing in the wind, wind chimes, and horns honking. Let your puppy play in and around empty boxes, tunnels, or buckets. Allow him to investigate trees, rocks, bushes, branches, leaves, and fallen fruit. He should explore bugs, and other animal odors, pastures, wooded areas, city sidewalks, and sandy beaches.

Enlarge your puppy's world and challenge his curiosity by taking him for rides in the car and walks in the park. Take him to the bank, post office, flower shop, veterinarian's office, and outdoor cafe for a cookie and a kiss.

As your puppy's guardian, protect him from potentially harmful or fearful situations, but don't coddle or reward fearful behavior. Observe your puppy's reactions to different situations. Watch his ears, tail, and body posture. Is he fearful? Apprehensive? Courageous? Dominant? Submissive? By understanding and reading your Aussie's body language, you can evaluate and adjust the situation accordingly. If your Aussie was raised in a childless environment, a room full of noisy, rambunctious children may be overwhelming or downright scary. By coddling or otherwise rewarding a puppy who shows fear, you reinforce that fear. Modify or restrict the exposure to one quiet, well-behaved child, until your puppy's confidence can handle more. When your puppy is brave, praise and reinforce him for being brave and inquisitive. "Good puppy!" or "Look at you. Aren't you brave!"

If you do nothing else for your puppy, you owe it to him to make the time to properly and adequately socialize him during this critical life stage. Yes, it's time consuming, but it is a necessary and obligatory investment when you choose to own an Australian Shepherd. His future well being depends on how much you do—or fail to do—during this critical period.

CRATE TRAINING

When used properly by responsible dog owners, a crate is an excellent training tool. While many owners look upon a crate as cruel or inhumane, it really should be viewed from a dog's perspective. Before dogs became domesticated pets, they tended to seek safe, enclosed areas for security and protection. A crate mimics that safe, enclosed environment. Puppies, especially very young puppies, tire quickly and need a lot of sleep during the day. A crate placed in a quiet corner of the kitchen or family room will satisfy a dog's natural instinct to seek a safe and secure environment. When properly introduced, a crate becomes a safe-zone for your Australian Shepherd—a quiet place all his own to sleep, eat, and retreat from the demands of being a puppy.

What's So Great About a Crate?

A key to successful puppy rearing is to never put your puppy in a position where he can get himself into trouble. Any puppy left unsupervised will develop bad habits. In record time, your adorable Australian Shepherd puppy can pee on the carpet, ransack the trash, and gnaw the leg off your antique armoire. Does the expression, "I just turned my back for a second!" sound familiar? During those short periods when you cannot watch your puppy closely, a crate prevents him from getting into mischief.

A crate is one of the safest, most successful, and efficient ways to housetrain a young puppy or adult dog. If your Aussie has an accident in his crate, the mess is much easier to clean and less damaging than when it is in the middle of your expensive Persian rug.

A crate is also ideal for keeping your Aussie safe while traveling.

A crate is an excellent tool for housetraining your puppy.

A crated dog will not distract you from your driving responsibilities, teethe on your armrests, chew on your designer purse, ransack the grocery bags, try to snatch that tasty burger from the cashier at the drive-up window, or eat your cell phone. Many motels and hotels, as well as friends and family, are more receptive to dogs when they are crate trained. As your Aussie grows and matures, the crate will continue to be his den and safe place for eating, sleeping, and retreating from the often chaotic and noisy world of humans.

How to Crate Train Your Australian Shepherd

A crate, like any other training tool, has the potential to be abused. A crate is not intended for 24-hour confinement. Your Australian Shepherd should live with you and not in his crate. A crate should never be used as a form of punishment. It should provide your Aussie with a safe, secure environment. A place your Aussie enjoys.

Most puppies quickly learn to love their crate when it is associated with good things, such as feeding, yummy treats, security, and sleep. To maximize the crate training process:

- Make the crate attractive to your puppy by placing an old blanket, towel, or rug and a few of his favorite indestructible chew toys inside the crate. Remember, young puppies love to chew, so choose toys and blankets that are safe and do not present a potential choking hazard.
- Leave the crate door open and allow your puppy to explore in and around the crate. If your puppy goes inside the crate, praise him. "Good puppy!" or "Aren't you clever!" Reward him with a tasty tidbit while he is in the crate.
- If your puppy is reluctant to go inside, encourage him by letting him see you toss a tasty tidbit of food inside the crate, preferably toward the back. When your puppy goes inside the crate to retrieve the food, praise him. "Good puppy!"
- Feed your puppy his meals inside the crate, luring him inside

with his food bowl. This makes the crate a positive place for your puppy to be.

- When your puppy is comfortable being inside the crate, and shows no signs of stress, try closing the door for 1 minute. Open the door and praise your puppy for being brave! "Look at you! You're so brave!"
- As your puppy becomes more comfortable with the crate, gradually increase the time he spends there. Never confine him for longer than 1 hour at a time—except at night when he is sleeping.
- If your puppy whines or cries, avoid reinforcing the behavior by letting him out of the crate or coddling him, such as saying, "What's the matter, baby?" Wait for him to be quiet for a minute or two before opening the door (provided you are certain he does not need to relieve himself).

HOUSETRAINING

The object of housetraining is to teach your puppy to relieve himself outdoors and not on your floors. As a general rule, Aussies are no more difficult to housetrain than any other dog. Some puppies can be more difficult to housetrain than others, but that has more to do with the individual puppy, rather than the breed. The key to successful housetraining is commitment, vigilance, and consistency on the part of the owner.

Housetraining is a relatively easy and painless process, yet it often causes owners a great deal of anxiety. Good planning and preparation and your unwavering commitment to the situation will provide your puppy with the best possible start. Crate training, when done properly, helps quickly and efficiently housetrain a puppy. If your puppy was born in the wild, most likely he would live in a cave or den, and most den animals have an instinctive desire to keep their dens clean. As a result, they avoid eliminating in their den. A crate serves as your puppy's den. If you watch a litter of puppies, you will notice that around 3 weeks of age the puppies will begin moving away from the whelping box to relieve themselves. A dog's deep-seated instinct to keep his den clean provides the foundation of housetraining via use of a crate. If you take advantage of this natural instinct, you reduce the chance of accidents. As your puppy matures, gradually teach him to hold his bladder for longer periods of time.

Working All Day?

If you are working and cannot let your puppy out every hour, try using a playpen or exercise pen to confine him. This will give your puppy room to play, exercise, and relieve himself if necessary.

Around 3 weeks of age the puppies will begin moving away from the whelping box to relieve themselves.

To increase your chances of success while minimizing accidents, provide your puppy with a regular schedule of eating, sleeping, and eliminating. Dogs are creatures of habit, and your Aussie will have an easier time adjusting to his new household and a housetraining schedule if you establish some order and routine to his life.

Understanding Your Puppy

The first step in any successful housetraining program is recognizing that young puppies have very little or no bladder control until around 5 months of age. Puppies mature at different rates, so your puppy's control may develop earlier or later. A 7- or 8-week-old puppy is equivalent to a 4- or 6-month-old human baby. You would not expect a young baby to control his bladder, and it is unfair to ask your puppy to exercise control that he does not have.

Puppies are most active during the day—running, jumping, training, playing, exploring, and being a puppy. Because of their limited bladder size and lack of control, it goes without saying that they are going to need to relieve themselves many, many times throughout the day. During the night, however, puppies are usually exhausted from their busy day of being a puppy. They are more relaxed and, as a result, most puppies can sleep between 5 and 8 hours without having to potty. This varies from puppy to puppy and, in this sense, they are not unlike human babies. Some parents get lucky and their babies sleep through the night. Others are

Housetraining Quick Tip

As a general rule, puppies need to relieve themselves 15 to 20 minutes after drinking, and 30 minutes to 1 hour after eating. Pay attention to when your puppy eats and drinks, and what he's doing each time he relieves himself. Knowing what is normal behavior for your puppy means you will know when something is haywire.

relegated to months of sleeplessness.

If your puppy wakes you up in the middle of the night or early in the morning because he needs to go, it is always better to get up with him. The fewer accidents he has in his crate, the less stressful the process will be and, while it may seem like forever, it will not be long before he can hold on all night.

Setting Up a Schedule

For the first several months—until your puppy begins to develop some reliable bladder control—you must take him outdoors frequently. When you are 100 percent committed to a regular schedule, your puppy quickly learns that relieving himself occurs on schedule.

As a general guideline—to increase your chances of success while minimizing accidents—take your puppy outdoors at the following times:

- First thing in the morning when he wakes up, and at least once every hour throughout the day.
- About 15 minutes after drinking water.
- About 30 minutes after eating.
- Immediately after waking from a nap.
- When you arrive home.
- Any time you take him out of his crate.
- Anytime he shows signs of having to go.
- Last thing at night.

This guideline is for young puppies. Because puppies are individuals and must be treated as such, you may need to tweak or adjust this schedule to fit your puppy's individual needs. No one said raising a puppy was all fun and no work! Housetraining a puppy is a time-consuming endeavor, but time invested at this stage will make your life easier in the long run. It may seem unnecessary to take your puppy outside every hour to potty, but taking him out on a regular basis is easier, cheaper, and less aggravating than constantly cleaning or replacing carpets. Dogs are either housetrained or they aren't—the fewer mistakes your Aussie has as a puppy, the faster he will learn to relieve himself outdoors, making him a more reliable adult dog. It is worth noting that these steps work equally well when housetraining an adult dog—especially if you have acquired a rescue or shelter dog. In these instances, it is always wise to assume he is not housetrained and begin the

What to Do at Night

If your puppy wakes you up when he has to go, and you find you simply cannot get up several times during the night—cover an area of the floor with sheets of newspaper. This works particularly well in a kitchen, which usually has a vinyl or linoleum floor. Set up an exercise pen on top of the newspaper and put his crate inside the exercise pen. At night, leave his crate door open. He will have access to his crate for sleeping, and he can also potty on the paper if he needs to go. The exercise pen will keep him confined to a small area.

This technique works in a pinch. However, it is always worthwhile to make the effort to get up with your puppy if he needs to go outside, because teaching your puppy to urinate indoors on newspaper creates its own set of problems.

For successful housetraining, it's important to set up a schedule and stick to it.

housetraining process as if he were a puppy.

How to Housetrain Your Australian Shepherd

First thing each morning, when you hear that unmistakable "I gotta go" whimper, let your puppy out of his crate and immediately take him outdoors to a designated spot. Do not procrastinate or allow yourself to get sidetracked making coffee, checking your e-mail, or fumbling around for a leash—keep one in a convenient spot. A few seemingly insignificant minutes to you is long enough to guarantee an accident for your puppy. Remember, your puppy has limited bladder control, and he's been confined in his crate for several hours. He simply can't wait another 2 or 3 minutes while you brush your teeth. He needs to go right now!

While you are outside, watch your puppy to make sure he empties his bladder or bowels. It may take a few minutes, so be patient. When your puppy has finished doing his business, calmly praise: "Good puppy!" or "Good potty!" Once you have seen your puppy relieve himself outdoors, you can allow him supervised play indoors. If you take your puppy outdoors and he does not relieve himself, it is important that you put him back in his crate for 5 or 10 minutes and then repeat the aforementioned steps. (If you are not using a crate to housetrain, keep your puppy where you can watch him like a hawk for those 5 or 10 minutes.) Do this as many times as necessary until your puppy relieves himself outdoors. Never assume your puppy has done his business. You must see your puppy empty his bladder or bowels. You need to repeat this routine many, many times throughout the day and again just before you go to bed at night.

Why Do I Have to Go Outside with Him?

Why go to all this trouble? Going out with your puppy and seeing him relieve himself serves many important purposes. First, if your puppy is on leash, you can take him to the same spot each time he needs to eliminate. This helps establish the habit of using a certain area of your yard. This also helps to keep your puppy on track and prevent him from getting too distracted with the potpourri of sights, smells, and sounds. Puppies are naturally curious and easily distracted, but if your puppy gets too distracted and forgets to go, when you bring him back indoors and he is no longer distracted, he will feel a sudden urge to go and the odds are good that he will go on your carpet.

Young puppies, generally under the age of 3 months, find comfort and security by being close to you. If you leave while your puppy is searching for a spot to potty, he will likely run after you and forget about the task at hand. If you put him outdoors and leave him to his own devices, he's likely to spend most of his time trying to get back in the house to be with you and, again, he will have forgotten about the task at hand. If you bring him indoors and he hasn't relieved himself outdoors—guess where he's going to potty?

In addition, by going outside with your puppy, you can praise him for doing what you want, which is going to the bathroom outdoors. This helps your puppy to understand exactly what you want, thereby maximizing the learning process.

Look for the Signs

Owners often run amok by thinking their puppy is housetrained when it is only wishful thinking on their part. Puppies between the ages of 8 and 10 weeks do not show signs of having to urinate. When they have to go, they go right away—often stopping to urinate in the middle of their play session. It is unrealistic to expect your puppy to stop what he is doing and tell you when he needs to go outside. More often than not, your puppy will not realize he has to go until he is already going. Your job for the next 6 months, or longer depending on the puppy, is to keep an eye on your puppy and anticipate his bathroom needs.

Around 10 or 12 weeks of age, a puppy will start to exhibit signs—warning signals that he is about to urinate or defecate—by circling, making crying noises, sniffing the floor, arching his back, or standing by the door. This is where owners get over confident

Housetraining Quick Tip

Limit your puppy's food and water intake approximately 1 hour before you turn out the lights. This helps to ensure his bladder and bowels are empty. **Note:** Do not restrict water intake during the day, but don't allow your puppy to drink heavily as bedtime approaches.

Adding a Verbal Cue

By going with your puppy, you can also begin instilling a verbal cue for the command, such as "Go pee" or "Go potty." A notable English trainer likes to use the cue "Go whiz!" You can choose a separate word for urinating and defecating. Whatever cue words you choose, be sure they are words you are comfortable using for many years. Some words might be funny in the confines of your home, but in public they may be a tad bit embarrassing. These verbal cues should be given each time your puppy is in the *process* of urinating or defecating, otherwise you will teach him the wrong association. The words should be said in a calm but encouraging tone of voice. If your voice is too excitable, your puppy is likely to forget what he is doing and run to see what you are so excited about.

and think they are home free. These are signs that your puppy is learning, not that he is housetrained. Now more than ever you need to remain diligent and stick to the program. Teach him which signal to use when he needs to go outside by reinforcing any or all of the signals. If he stands by the door, take him outdoors. If he relieves himself outside, praise him. "Good potty!"

By following these simple steps, your Aussie learns through repetition and consistency to relieve himself outdoors. Patience and consistency are the keys to housetraining. There are no short cuts, and you mustn't become complacent. Doing so will only create problems that will exist for many years to come. The more your puppy can do his business outdoors, the quicker he will learn, the happier you will be, and the sooner the entire family can get back to being barefoot in the house!

Accidents Will Happen

It is in yours and your dog's best interest to keep indoor accidents to a minimum. However, few Aussie owners escape puppy rearing without an accident here or there. If an accident does happen, consider it your fault and resign yourself to being more observant in the future. Never scold or hit your puppy and never, ever rub his nose in the mess. Those are not housetraining techniques—they are crimes in progress. Punishing, yelling, or otherwise berating your puppy will only confuse him and prolong the housetraining process.

Dogs live in the moment. Young or old, they do not have the mental wherewithal to associate the punishment they are receiving with an earlier act of urinating on the floor. When you scold your puppy, he will display a submissive response. Your puppy is reacting to your mannerisms and tone of voice. Most owners tend to believe their puppy's submissive demeanor is because he understands he did something wrong. They often say, "He knows what he did wrong. He even looks guilty!"

Scolding, punishing, or berating your puppy is counterproductive to building a solid, trusting, and mutually respectful relationship. A puppy who lives in fear of you is likely to grow into an adult dog who is anxious and frequently worried. If he potty's on the floor, and you scold him when you get home 10 minutes or 2 hours later, he is likely to become anxious and perhaps fearful of being left alone, which can exacerbate urinating in the house or cause him to develop all sorts of unwanted behaviors

Bring your puppy outside to relieve himself regularly.

as he grows into an adult dog. Be smart. Stick to a reliable housetraining protocol.

TRAINING YOUR AUSTRALIAN SHEPHERD

Puppies and adult dogs learn through repetition and consistency. To provide your puppy with a basic foundation of obedience skills and manners that allow him to grow into a well-behaved adult dog and co-exist with humans, be consistent with your expectations. Aussies learn faster when the rules stay the same.

It is very important that your Aussie trusts you and not feel he must worry about how you are going to react from day to day. It is unfair to allow an 8-week-old puppy to jump on you today, but scold him for doing so tomorrow, when his feet are muddy. He does not understand his feet are muddy and your designer skirt is expensive. If you do not want your adult Aussie jumping on you, discourage the behavior while he is a young, impressionable puppy. It is equally unfair to allow your adorable puppy on the

furniture today, but reprimand him for the same behavior when he is a 50-pound (22.5 kg) adult dog. It is unfair to feed your dog at the table every night, then act mortified and correct him when he begs your in-laws for tidbits of steak and potatoes. Think ahead, and decide which behaviors you will or will not accept and which behaviors you can or cannot live with for the next 12 to 15 years.

Dogs Are Individuals

Equally important in the training process is understanding that all puppies are individuals. A litter of puppies may look alike, but each has his own unique character, temperament, and personality. As a result of each dog's genetic makeup, plus some environmental influences, each will grow into an adult dog who possesses his own distinct qualities.

If you have children, think how each was raised with the same amount of love, individual attention, rules, and values to make the most of their personalities and talents. Yet despite their seemingly uniform upbringing, each child is an individual with his own special talents, likes, dislikes, quirks, and idiosyncrasies.

A keen understanding of the Australian Shepherd breed—his history and origin—will help you to better understand what makes your puppy tick. Get in the habit of watching your puppy when he is sleeping, playing by himself or with other animals or with children. Is he bold? Sassy? Bossy? Does he growl or attack other animals? Does he cower from children? Is he inquisitive? Is he full of energy?

Understanding your puppy's individual personality helps you to recognize which behaviors you can live with and which might preclude a long and happy human–canine relationship. If your puppy is bossy and pushy, begin right away discouraging the behavior of bolting out doors or grabbing food or toys from your hand without permission. If your puppy is shy or nervous, expose him to safe situations that will help build his confidence, such as encouraging friends to get on the ground and talk to him, play with him, rub his tummy, and kiss his nose. Take him for rides in the car or trips to the neighbor's barn—on leash, of course—to see the horses and explore strange smells, sights, and sounds.

What Type of Training Is Best for My Aussie?

Many wonderful methods are available for training puppies and adult dogs. The hardest part is deciphering between the enormous variety of training methods and trainers. What works, what doesn't? Who's right, who's wrong? In today's canine-friendly environment, it seems that as many trainers and training methods exist as breeds of dogs. Positive and negative motivation, food training, play training, toy training, and clicker training—throw in the endless variety of paraphernalia employed, from electronic gizmos to metallic gadgetry—and the entire process can seem more complicated than computer science.

The good news is that Australian Shepherds are highly trainable and quick to learn, and raising and training an Aussie is not terribly difficult. It is well within the capabilities of most dog owners who set their mind to it. It does, however, require time, insight, dedication, and the ability to view setbacks with a sense of humor. Aussies are intelligent. Most love to please their owners, but they do not like to be bullied or browbeaten. Berating them or treating them harshly will not get you far. They are likely to tune you out and give up trying. Some Aussies have been known to hold a grudge, too. They must be trained and handled with respect, fairness, and consistency.

Successful Training

Successful training includes having a clear picture of what you want to accomplish and a well-thought-out game plan, which includes regular training, socialization, and interaction with your puppy both at home and in public. Additionally, it helps if you start right away—preferably as soon as your Aussie starts living with you.

Years ago, the accepted methodology of dog training was that a puppy had to be at least 6 months old before you began teaching basic obedience skills. That concept has since been debunked; modern-day breeders, trainers, and animal behaviorists now recognize the important benefits of early training—as early as 8 weeks of age. Additionally, past trainers often employed the standard pop-and-jerk type training that involved a choke chain, force, and a total domination of the dog. While that method usually produced desired results, it often came at a hefty price that included stifling a dog's personality as well as his willingness and desire to please.

Today's top trainers had the foresight and willingness to change by recognizing the importance of allowing dogs and handlers to

Managing His Environment

Only rarely—if ever—should you discipline or correct a young puppy. The majority of your interactions should be positive and fun as you work toward building a solid human–canine relationship by instilling desired behaviors, discouraging undesired behaviors, and fostering his personality. Managing your Aussie so he does not develop bad habits is critical. Take every opportunity to manipulate the situations so that your dog does the right thing and can be rewarded—the essence of positive motivation. If left to their own devices, Aussies, like most dogs, will do what is in their best interest and that is seldom, if ever, conducive to living in a domesticated environment.

Training with food rewards is a positive way to teach your Aussie.

be themselves, rather than imposing the same training method regardless of temperament. While trainers still exist who adhere to the ideology of force and domination as a means of training, most trainers today employ gentler training methods that include praise, positive motivation, and positive reinforcement.

The concept behind positive motivation and reinforcement is that when a behavior has favorable consequences the probability that the behavior will be repeated is increased. A dog learns to repeat a behavior, such as sit, down, or come, to receive a reward. The reward can be a combination of verbal or physical praise coupled with a tasty tidbit of food or his favorite toy.

Puppy Kindergarten

If your Australian Shepherd is between 2 and 5 months of age, a puppy kindergarten class is an ideal environment for exposing and socializing him to the many things he will encounter in his adult life. Puppy classes help your Aussie continue to expand on his knowledge of canine communication and social skills that he learned from his mother and while interacting with his littermates. A puppy class allows him to continue learning to communicate and interact with other dogs in a low-risk and stress-free environment.

Puppy classes should not be a free-for-all, where puppies play on their own while their owners socialize on the sidelines. A well-structured puppy class will begin teaching basic obedience skills, including fun puppy recall games, sit, down, and name recognition. You will learn how to read canine body language, how to train your puppy, and how to recognize problems early on, before they become annoying, ingrained habits that are difficult to break.

LEASH TRAINING

Walking an adult Australian Shepherd who constantly pulls and lunges against his leash is a frustrating challenge for even the most patient (and strongest!) owners.

The formal Heel command is used by most obedience

competitors, who are sticklers for precision. They spend years teaching their dogs to walk with their head and body in a specific position. Most Aussie owners are not going to require that much precision. They are quite happy if their dog is not dragging them down the street.

While the traditional heel position is on the handler's left side, there may be times when you won't care if your dog is on your left, right, or walking out in front of you. That said, it is always easier to teach your puppy to walk on leash by starting on the left side and sticking with it until he understands the exercise. Once he has mastered walking nicely on leash, you can allow him to walk on the right or out in front of you.

Leash Training Puppies

It is vital that your puppy not associate his leash and collar with a barrage of corrections or nagging. He should view walking on leash as something fun that he does with his owner.

To begin:

- Always teach this exercise on a buckle collar, never a choke-chain.

Keep It Fun!

Maximize your dog's training by avoiding techniques that are repetitious, predictable, and boring for your dog. Australian Shepherds are intelligent, quick to learn, and always ready for a game. As a result, they can also become bored quite quickly, too. Use your imagination. Be creative and come up with fun training techniques and games that stimulate your Aussie's mind and increase his desire to learn.

Finding a Trainer

To find the right trainer or puppy class for you and your Australian Shepherd:

- Ask your veterinarian, breeder, dog groomer, or dog-owning friends for referrals. Word-of-mouth is a great tool for uncovering talented and knowledgeable trainers, and avoiding problem ones.
- Contact professional organizations that certify or recommend trainers, such as the Association of Pet Dog Trainers or National Association of Dog Obedience Instructors.
- Attend the classes of several trainers to observe their personalities, training techniques, and facilities.
- Look for trainers who focus on rewarding what your Aussie does right rather than punishing what he does wrong.
- Does the trainer recognize that puppies are individuals? Are the same training methods imposed on all the puppies, regardless of their breed and mental maturity?
- Puppies learn best in low-risk, stress-free environments. Look for classes that are structured, run smoothly, and emphasize fun.
- Do the facilities provide a safe learning environment for you and your puppy? Are they well lit with matted floors and eight to ten puppies per class?
- Are the puppies separated—small puppies from large, young puppies from juniors, the rambunctious from the shy?
- Trust your instincts. Your puppy's safety and well-being are paramount. If you feel uncomfortable about the facility or trainer, find another puppy class.

In a dog show, dogs are moved on the handler's left side.

- Attach a leash (or thin long-line) to his collar and allow him to drag it around. Don't worry if he picks it up and tries to carry it around. In fact, put a command to the behavior. "Have you got your leash?" eventually becomes "Get your leash!"
- When your puppy is happily dragging the leash, pick it up and start walking forward, encouraging your puppy to walk close to your left by talking sweetly to him and luring him with a tasty tidbit from your left hand. (This is easier if the leash is in your right hand.)
- When you have walked a few steps with your dog on your left, reward him with the tidbit of food. Remember to verbally praise and offer the food reward when he is close beside your left leg. This encourages him to remain in position.
- Once your puppy is comfortable walking beside you, begin teaching a more formal "walk nicely on leash."

Walk Nicely on Leash

The goal is to teach your Aussie to walk nicely on leash—anywhere within the full extension of his leash, on either side of you, or in front of you—without pulling. He should also learn that a loose leash means he goes forward, which he's sure to find highly rewarding! Pulling on the leash means he stops...definitely nonrewarding! Puppies who learn not to yank their owner's shoulder out of the socket grow into adult dogs who do not pull on their leash. They are a joy to own because it is fun to take them for walks, and they are more likely to be included in family outings.

To begin:

1. Teach this exercise on a buckle collar, never on a choke chain.

2. With your puppy on leash, encourage him to stand close to your left leg by luring him into position with a tasty tidbit of food.

3. Praise and reward him with the tidbit when he gets there. "That's my boy!" (Teach a separate command for getting into position on your left side, such as "Close" or "With me." When he is in the position you want, for example, on your left, reward him with the tidbit and praise, "That's your Close" or "Good Close!" Eventually, the dog will learn to associate "Close"—or whatever command you choose—with being in position on your left.)

4. Show him the tidbit of food. When you have his attention, hold the food ever so slightly above his nose, just high enough that his head is up and he can nibble the food without jumping up. With the food in his face, say his name and give your command for walking on a loose leash (i.e., "Fido, let's go") and then start walking forward.

5. Keep your right hand (the one holding the leash) close to your body. This will keep the leash length consistent. As you walk forward, watch the leash. If it begins to tighten, stop walking and stand still. Most likely, your puppy will come to an abrupt halt and look back at you as if to say, "What the heck?"

6. Stand still and encourage your puppy back into position with the tidbit of food. Try to avoid moving or turning in circles to reposition your puppy. A dog cannot find your left side (i.e.,

Quick Tips for Leash Training Your Puppy

- Only reward sensible walking. If your puppy is jumping and lunging for the food, hold the food lower and in front of his nose, but do not give it to him until he takes two or three steps without jumping.
- If your puppy is not interested in following you—slow down and be more obvious with the lure. You may need to get a tastier lure, such as boiled chicken, wieners, liver, or leftover steak.
- If your puppy freezes on the spot and won't move, do not drag him around or force the issue. Try this: Drop the leash and run away while clapping your hands. Very young puppies like to follow their owners. Most likely, he will try to catch you. When he does, praise him for catching you. "Good boy!" Nonchalantly pick up the leash, start walking, and encourage him to walk close to your left side by luring him with a cookie and talking sweetly to him. Take two or three steps, praise, and reward.

heel position), if you're constantly moving.

7. When your puppy is repositioned on your left, repeat the above steps until he is walking beside you without pulling on the leash. When you have taken a few steps, stop, praise, and reward him while he is beside you. If you reward him when he is not in the correct position, you will have inadvertently taught him the wrong association.

8. When your puppy is walking beside you, tell him he is smart and clever. Chat sweetly to him to encourage him to walk beside you. Over time, gradually increase the number of steps he is walking on a loose leash, but try not to go so far that he gets out of position and begins pulling on the leash. The goal is to gradually increase the length of time between "Let's go" and rewarding with the treat.

In the beginning, treats are used to lure the dog into the correct position and show him what you want him to do. Once he understands walking nicely on leash, keep the treats in your pocket and reward him less often.

With a little paticene, your Aussie can learn to "walk nicely" by your side.

BASIC OBEDIENCE

The object of teaching basic obedience skills is to provide your Aussie with a set of commands he understands, thereby making your life and his more enjoyable. Trying to physically restrain a 50-pound (22.5 kg) Australian Shepherd who wants to zig when you want to zag is enough to make you wish you had bought a cat. An Australian Shepherd who does not have a solid foundation of canine manners and obedience skills can quickly grow into an unruly brat. An Australian Shepherd who is taught to respond reliably and quickly to basic commands is much easier and enjoyable to live with. No doubt, his life is more pleasurable because, as a well-behaved dog, he is more likely to be incorporated into the family environment, rather than relegated to the isolation of the backyard.

The Commands

The first step in teaching any exercise is to have a clear picture

Tips for Walking Nicely

- Always begin training in a familiar, quiet, and non-distractive environment. Your backyard, living room, or family room is ideal.
- Use random rewards and tasty tidbits (i.e., boiled chicken, leftover steak, turkey wieners) to keep your puppy interested and motivated.
- When first teaching this exercise, have a tidbit of food in your hand before starting. If you fumble in your pocket for food after your puppy has done an excellent job, he will be out of position and you will have lost the opportunity to reinforce the correct position. Remember, timing is everything when training dogs!
- Always dispense the food from your left hand. This keeps your puppy from crossing over in front of you—tripping you in the process—to get the tasty tidbit in your right hand.
- If you do your part when your puppy is young and still receptive to learning, then pulling and tugging on the leash is not a problem as he grows bigger and stronger.
- Teaching a puppy (or adult dog) to walk on leash takes time. Be patient. You will need to repeat these steps over and over before your dog gets the hang of it.

in your mind of what you want to teach. If you are teaching your Aussie to sit, have a clear picture in your mind of what a sit looks like. This may seem simple, if not downright silly, but if you cannot visualize it in your mind, how can you teach it and, more importantly, how can your dog learn it? Many owners have different ideas of what a sit or a down or even a come command represent. Some owners are happy if their dog comes on the eight or ninth command. Others want their Aussie to come the first time he is called. The choice is yours.

Dogs are naturally curious, and love to explore and test their boundaries. Therefore, begin your dog's training in a familiar environment that has a limited amount of distractions, such as your house or yard. This is especially helpful if you are training a young puppy.

Puppies have limited attentions spans and are easily distracted by kids playing, toys lying around, birds flying overhead, a bug on the ground, cows mooing, horses whinnying, and so forth. It is unreasonable to expect a young puppy to ignore all the distractions and focus entirely on you. "It's a bit like taking a child to Disneyland for the first time and expecting it to learn logarithms," says English dog trainer Annette Conn, and author of the book, *It's a Dog's Life*.

A dog who can respond to basic commands make a great family pet.

The Sit Command

Sit is a must-know command for every dog. A dog who understands the Sit command provides you with an avenue of control. Think of the many situations in which your Aussie will need to know how to sit—at the vet's office, waiting to be fed, waiting to cross the street, or sitting and waiting while you open any door. He will need to sit when you put his collar on or take it off, when you want to check his coat for stickers or burs, or when you want to brush him or trim his nails. The sit command increases his vocabulary and instills order in both your lives.

Teaching the sit command is relatively simple, and the guidelines are the same whether you are teaching a young puppy or an adult dog.

1. Begin with your puppy on leash. This is especially helpful if your dog, like most puppies, has his own agenda, tends to wander off, or is easily distracted.

2. Start with your leash in one hand, a tasty tidbit in the other hand, and your puppy standing in front of you. (Hold the tidbit firmly between your thumb and index finger so that your dog cannot get it until he is in the correct position.)

3. Show your puppy the tidbit by holding it close to and slightly above his nose. As your puppy raises his nose to take the food, slowly move the cookie in a slightly upward and backward direction toward his tail, keeping the cookie directly above his nose. (If your puppy jumps up or brings his front feet off

the ground, the cookie is too high. If he walks backwards, the cookie is too far back or too low.)

4. At this point, your puppy's hips should automatically sink toward the ground. As they do, give the Sit command. While your puppy is sitting, praise him with "Good sit!" and reward him with the tidbit. (Give the Sit command as your puppy's rear end hits the ground. Saying it too soon will teach the wrong association.)

5. Release your puppy with a release word, such as "Free" or "OK," play with him for a few seconds, and repeat the exercise three or four times in succession, three or four times a day.

The Down Command

Once your Aussie understands the Down command, you can use it when you are watching television, sewing, preparing dinner, reading quietly, or when friends come to visit and you do not want your dog directly involved in what you are doing at that moment. Your dog may need to lie down on the vet's exam table, while you brush or scratch his tummy, check his coat for stickers, or when you want to massage his sore muscles.

Teaching the Down command can be a bit more challenging than the Sit because it is considered a submissive position for some dogs. If your puppy has an independent personality, this exercise will take a bit more patience and persistence on your part. Do not give up! Remember, puppies learn through repetition and consistency.

Sit is one of the easiest commands to teach your Aussie.

1. Begin by kneeling on the floor so that you are eye level with your puppy.

2. With your puppy standing in front of you, hold a tasty tidbit of food in one hand.

3. Let your puppy sniff the cookie. Move the cookie toward the floor between his front feet.

4. When done correctly, your puppy will plant his front feet and fold his body into the Down position as he follows the cookie to the ground.

5. When his elbows and tummy are on the ground, give the command Down.

6. While your puppy is in the Down position,

- Get in the habit of saying the command one time. Avoid repeating yourself: "Sit, Sit, Sit, %#$@! SIT!" If you say it ten times, your Aussie will wait until the tenth command to respond.

- Make sure you give your puppy the release word before you allow him to rise out of the sit position. Doing so will clearly signal to the puppy the end of the exercise.

- Avoid saying "Sit down" when you really mean "Sit."

reward with the cookie and calmly praise: "Good down."

7. Release your puppy with a release word, such as "Free" or "OK," repeat the exercise three or four times in succession, three or four times a day.

The Sit-Stay Command

The goal of the Stay command is to teach your dog to stay in a specific position, such as in a sit or down, until you say it is OK to move. It is useful in a variety of situations, as when you want to answer or open the door without your Aussie bolting through it. To teach Sit-Stay:

1. Start with your puppy on a loose leash, sitting beside you.
2. Tell your puppy to Sit and to Stay. You can include a hand signal by holding the open palm of your hand in front of your puppy's face about 2 inches from his nose as you say "Stay."
3. Watch your dog closely for the slightest movement that may indicate he is about to stand up or lie down. Try to be proactive in your training by reminding your dog to stay before he moves.
4. Once he has remained in position for a few seconds, praise calmly and warmly with "Good stay" and a treat. Include calm, physical praise, such as gentle stroking—but not so enthusiastically that he gets excited and forgets the task at hand.
5. As soon as you see any movement, repeat your Stay command firmly, but not harshly.
6. If your dog stands up, use your leash to prevent him from moving away and get him into the Sit position again. If he lies down, gently reposition him and remind him to stay.
7. Reward him with a treat first, then release him with an "OK" or "Free" command. (If you release your dog first and then reward him, you will teach him the wrong association. He will think he is being rewarded for moving. This can teach a puppy to anticipate the reward, thereby encouraging him to break the Stay command.)

As your puppy matures and can remain sitting beside you for 2 or 3 minutes without moving, progress by giving the Stay command and then stepping directly in front of his nose. Gradually begin increasing the distance between you and your puppy.

Once you have a reliable Sit-Stay in a non-distractive situation, you can begin incorporating mild distractions, such as toys lying nearby on the floor. As your dog becomes reliable with mild distractions, begin escalating the distractions. Try training while other people or dogs play nearby. If your dog has a difficult time focusing on the task at hand, go back to a more non-distractive environment.

To teach the Down-Stay, begin with your dog in the Down position. Tell him to Stay. Then follow the remaining instructions for the Sit-Stay.

The Come Command

The goal is to teach your puppy to come to you reliably, willingly, and immediately—without hesitation—upon hearing the command, while in a wide range of situations, such as at the park, in the neighbor's yard, at a friend's house, in an emergency, or any time he gets loose. In your dog's mind, "Come" should never mean, "OK I hear you. I'll be there as soon as I finish chasing this bug." You want your dog to understand that when you say "Come!" it means, "Stop what you are doing and run back to me as fast as you can—right now." In the beginning, you teach this behavior with fun games and tasty rewards. Ideally, as he grows

Quick Tips: The Down

- Make sure you give your puppy a release word before you allow him to rise out of the down position. Doing so clearly signals to the dog the end of the exercise.

- Get in the habit of saying the command one time. Avoid repeating yourself: "Down, Down, Down, I said DOWN!" If you say it ten times, your Aussie will learn to wait until the tenth command to respond.

- Do not to use the command "Sit down" when you really mean "Down."

- Avoid confusing your dog by using the Down command when you really mean off—such as getting off the furniture or not jumping on you.

Teaching Down takes patience and persistence on your part.

into an adult dog, he comes because he wants to be with you—not just because you have a cookie. This is why it is so important to connect with him mentally—to establish a strong human–canine bond.

When Not to Use Come

Never use the Come command for anything your Aussie might dislike or to end playtime. When you call your puppy, do something silly with him when he gets to you, such as a quick game of tug, a fun trick, or reward him with a tasty tidbit, and then let him run off and play again. Owners often make the mistake of calling their puppy only when it is time to go in his kennel or to put his leash on and go home. In these situations, your puppy quickly learns that "Come" means the end of his freedom, and he is likely to avoid you the next time he is called.

Set Him Up to Succeed

When teaching the Come command, call your puppy only when you are absolutely certain he will respond. If you call your puppy when he is excited about greeting another dog, when a family member has just come to visit, or when he is eating his dinner, he will be too excited and distracted to respond to your command, and you will inadvertently be teaching him to ignore you. In the early stages, when your puppy is learning the Come command, wait until the excitement has subsided and then call him to you. If you must have your puppy during these times, it is better to go and get him rather than call him to you.

Quick Tips: The Stay

- Most Aussies are not emotionally mature enough to cope with this exercise until they are 5 or 6 months old. If this is the case with your puppy, do not force the issue. Simply wait until he is older and mentally more mature to understand and cope with the exercise.
- When first learning this command, 5 or 10 seconds in the Stay position is long enough for most dogs.
- Do not be in a hurry to move away from your dog or have him hold the position for longer periods.
- Do not nag, scold, send him threatening looks, or make impatient snorting noises during a Stay. Dogs who are bullied or intimidated into staying are less reliable in the long run. Dogs learn faster and retain more information when they learn in a stress-free environment.
- Never leave your dog in a Stay position unsupervised, such as outside a store or anywhere he could run off, be hurt, stolen, or lost.

Teach Come in an enclosed space.

Equally important, take advantage of opportunities in which you can set him up to succeed by calling him back to you when he would be coming to you anyway, such as when you have just arrived home and he is running toward you, or when you have his dinner or a tasty tidbit. Let him know how clever he is when he gets to you. "What a good come!"

A puppy who views Come as a fun game is more likely to develop a reliable response to the command. If this behavior continues throughout his puppyhood, and you remain excited and enthusiastic each and every time he comes to you, you will have a strong and positive response to the behavior as he matures into an adult dog.

Start by Teaching Find Me

Your can use an informal game like Find Me! to begin teaching Come in a positive, fun, and exciting manner. This game capitalizes on a dog's natural chase instinct. It is also an excellent game for instilling the Come command in young puppies.

1. Start with a pocket full of tasty tidbits.
2. Rev your puppy up by showing him a yummy treat and then toss the treat down the hallway or across the living room.
3. As your puppy runs for the cookie, you run in the opposite direction and hide behind a chair or door as you say his name enthusiastically.
4. When your puppy finds you, make a big fuss: Get on the floor,

roll around, and lavish him with a potpourri of kisses and praise. "Good come!" or "You found me!"

5. Repeat the game several times throughout the day, but not so many times that your dog becomes bored.

You can also play this game outdoors. Be sure to play in a fenced area to protect your dog from harm or prevent him from running off. When you are outside in your yard with your dog and he stops to sniff the grass or explore a bug—duck behind a tree or bush, clap your hands and say his name in an exciting tone of voice.

When your dog gets to you, greet him with plenty of hugs, kisses, and praise, "Good come!" or "Good boy!" It is not necessary for your dog to sit before he gets a treat. If you insist on your puppy sitting first, you will not be rewarding the most important part of the exercise, which is coming to you.

PROBLEM BEHAVIORS

In a perfect world, puppies and adult dogs would never get into trouble! In the real world, however, it is unrealistic to expect any dog to go through his entire life without getting into some sort of mischief or developing an annoying habit or two. Remember that dogs, like kids, are first and foremost individuals. No two are alike, and they must be treated as individuals to maximize their potential. Their temperaments will fall within a broad range of characteristics, and they will develop their own quirks and idiosyncrasies.

That said, annoying or offensive behaviors do not suddenly appear—they are learned. Dogs do not do anything you do not

Quick Tips for Come

- Your Aussie must always chase you. Avoid making a game of you chasing your dog, and never allow kids to chase your dog. It inadvertently teaches him to run away from you, which creates many, many problems down the road.

- If your puppy comes to you, you must always, always, always praise him—even if moments before he chewed your shoes, urinated on the floor, or ransacked the trash. There are no exceptions to this rule.

- Never call "Come" and then correct him for something he did, such as chewing your shoe or urinating on the floor. Punishing him when he gets to you will only make it less likely that he will come back the next time. If you need to correct your dog, go and get him. Never call him to you.

- Do not call "Come" if you want to give him a bath, administer medications, or do anything else he might find unpleasant. Instead, go and get your dog; then put him in the tub, trim his nails, administer medications, etc.

- Never allow your puppy to run off leash in an unfenced or unconfined area. Doing so puts your puppy at risk and teaches him bad habits because he is too young to reliably respond to the Come command.

allow to happen. Puppies and adult dogs do not pee from one end of the house to the other just to annoy you. Their brains are not hardwired to be vindictive. If your dog is urinating in the house, it is because he is not housetrained, and he is not being supervised.

Equally important, puppies do not magically outgrow problems. A puppy who digs holes in your garden will not suddenly stop digging, regardless of how much you hope and pray. If you do not want him digging up your favorite roses, modify his environment so that he is not put in a position where he is allowed to get himself into trouble.

Barking (Excessive)

Overall, the Australian Shepherd is not a noisy dog, and excessive or chronic barking is generally not a problem. However, many Aussies do like to vocalize and backchat, and they need to be taught to stop barking on command. It is natural for dogs to bark or otherwise vocalize, and they do so for a variety of reasons. They bark when they get excited, when playing with other dogs, when the doorbell rings, and to greet you when you arrive home. If you have done enough proper socialization, your Aussie should not regard every little noise as an endless opportunity to bark.

Many Aussies have an innate ability to protect their territory and will alert bark without being taught to do so. Your Aussie's barking is reasonable and appropriate if he is alerting you to suspicious intruders or unexpected visitors. If you can quiet him with a single command (or two!), you probably do not have much to worry about. Problems arise when your dog is too hyped up to stop barking. For this reason, it is best to curtail any problems immediately. This includes never encouraging your Aussie to bark. For example, when the doorbell rings, avoid asking your dog, "Who's there?" or "Let's go see!" This can excite your Aussie and encourage him to bark. It may seem like a fun game when he is 10 or 12 weeks old, but it is a difficult and annoying behavior to stop once it becomes ingrained.

If your puppy is barking as an attention-seeking behavior, ignore him until he quiets. Then calmly praise, "Good Quiet!" or "Good Boy!" Resist the urge to verbally or physically acknowledge your dog's barking by shouting "NO!" or "SHUT UP!" This only encourages the unwanted behavior because, in your dog's mind, negative attention is better than no attention at all. By verbally

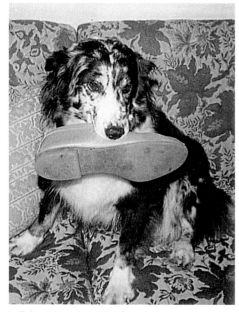

All dogs get into mischief now and then—it's your job to supervise and not allow bad habits to develop.

responding to your dog, you are inadvertently giving him what he wants: attention.

Avoid soothing or otherwise coddling your Aussie when he is barking. This too inadvertently encourages the unwanted behavior. If your dog is barking, and you tell him, "It's okay, honey. Mommy loves you," the dog thinks he is being rewarded for barking. He thinks, "When I bark, my mom tells me it's okay. So I should keep barking."

Most barking problems can be avoided if you plan ahead, having a clear picture of the behaviors you will and will not accept. However, if your Australian Shepherd has already developed a barking problem and is well on his way to wearing out his welcome, try a shaker can as a training aid, coupled with positive reinforcement.

Using a Shaker Can

Shaker cans make a lot of noise, and that's what you want! The concept is that the noise from the shaker can interrupts your dog's barking and, once the dog's barking behavior is interrupted, you can praise and reward him for not barking.

Shaker cans are easy to make—simply fill an empty soda can with a dozen or so coins or small pebbles and tape the opening closed. As soon as your Australian Shepherd begins to bark—for example, when the doorbell rings—immediately give a command, such as "Quiet," "Enough," or "No Bark," and shake the can. If done correctly, the noise should be loud enough to startle the dog and interrupt his barking. When he stops barking, immediately praise: "Good Quiet!" or "Good Boy!" Reinforce the behavior with a tidbit of food, but do so only when the dog is not barking. Otherwise, you will teach the wrong association and inadvertently reinforce the barking.

Keep multiple shaker cans strategically placed around the house—near the telephone, front door, bedroom, living, room, etc.—for convenience and accessibility. Have shaker cans strategically located outdoors, as well.

A word of caution: Place shaker cans out of your Aussie's reach. Aluminum cans are sharp and dangerous when punctured or torn. Aussies, curious creatures that they are, can cause serious damage to their teeth, tongues, mouths, and stomachs if they chew on the can. Once an Aussie gets the can open, he may try to swallow the coins, which presents a potential choking hazard. Most important, never throw the can—or any other objects—at your Aussie. You may injure or frighten him, and he will most likely learn to fear you.

Smart Dog Management

The best prevention against future barking problems is smart dog management.

Never allow your puppy or adult Aussie to be put in a situation in which he is allowed to develop bad habits. This includes leaving him in the backyard unsupervised all day, where he is inspired to bark at constant stimuli like other dogs barking, a cat on a fence, a bird overhead, leaves falling, neighbors coming and going, and life in general.

Barking at environmental stimulation is often self-rewarding for the dog. A dog barks at the postman and, when the postman leaves, the dog thinks, "Look how clever I am! My barking made that man leave!"

An Aussie housed indoors can also develop barking habits. If he sits on the furniture and stares out the living room window, he may be encouraged to bark at stimuli, such as neighbors, other dogs going for a walk, kids on bicycles, or the UPS man.

If your dog barks during the excitement of play—stop the game immediately. When your dog stops barking, praise: "Good Quiet!" or "Good Boy!" Once you have regained control of the situation, begin playing again.

Chewing

It is hard to imagine an adorable 10-week-old Aussie puppy as a one-dog demolition team. However, do not let his cute looks deceive you. Aussie puppies, like most puppies, can be incredibly aggressive chewers and wreak havoc in your household. They can destroy

Excessive barking may be a sign of loneliness or boredom.

drywall, carpet, drapes, and linoleum. They can turn your favorite pillows into confetti, shred your bedspread, destroy electrical cords, and potted plants. They will gleefully shred magazines, books, and anything else they can get their teeth on—and that's in the 15 minutes it takes you to drive to the post office and back!

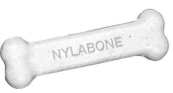

If you must leave—even for 2 minutes—take your Aussie with you or confine him in a crate, exercise pen, or kennel. Do not put your puppy in a situation where he can develop bad habits. This point cannot be emphasized enough. Puppies chew, especially when they are teething.

Prevention Is Key

Few escape canine ownership without losing a slipper, a pair of rubber golashes, or a potted plant. Puppies are going to chew. It is a fact of life. However, the key to minimizing destruction and preventing bad habits is management. Any puppy left unsupervised is trouble looking for someplace to happen.

If you allow your puppy free run of the house, do not be surprised when you come home to find epic amounts of destruction. It is equally unfair to scold or otherwise punish a puppy for your temporary lapse of good judgment. Therefore, to foster good habits and minimize destructive behaviors, follow these simple guidelines:

Before bringing your new puppy home, plan ahead. Have an exercise pen or play pen and a crate ready. Do not wait until you think you need them. If you have an Aussie, you need them.

When you cannot keep a constant watch on your puppy, keep

Tips for Problem Barkers

These tips will help enhance your chances of success:
- Consistency and timing are keys to success. Be consistent each time your dog barks, until you can train him to respond to your Quiet or No Bark command.
- Positive reinforcement is much more productive than negative reinforcement. Verbally praise and reward the behavior you want, which is your dog not barking.
- Dogs learn an appropriate alternative to barking when you are there to teach them. If you are seldom home, you cannot expect them to learn on their own.
- Dogs are individuals. They learn at different rates. You may see improvement within a few days—or it may take many weeks. Remember, Rome wasn't built in a day!

him confined in an exercise pen, play pen, crate, or puppy-proofed area with his favorite chew toy. This includes when you need to jump in the shower for 5 minutes, while you are making dinner, or when you dash outside for 2 seconds to move the sprinkler.

Once your puppy arrives at your home, know where he is and what he is doing at all times. You would not dream of taking your eyes off a toddler, and you should never take your eyes off an Aussie puppy when he is not safely confined.

Puppy-proof your home. Puppies are ingenious when it comes to finding items to chew on. Pick up anything and everything your puppy is likely to put in his mouth including shoes, purses, jackets, schoolbooks, candles, rugs, electrical cords, dolls, and so forth.

Make sure your Aussie receives plenty of exercise each day. Puppies and adult dogs require daily physical and mental stimulation. Lacking appropriate and adequate exercise, they will release pent up energy through chewing, digging, or barking.

The Importance of Chew Toys

A variety of chew toys are available in all sizes and shapes to entertain your Australian Shepherd for an hour or two. Chew toys such as Nylabones will satisfy your puppy's need to gnaw on something, while diverting him from chewing on inappropriate items. While some chew toys are better than others, there is no scientific formula for finding the right chew toy. Most times, it is a matter of trial and error. Avoid toys or bones that are too hard and may crack your dog's teeth, or those that are too small or break apart and present choking hazards.

Chews are available in a wide variety of shapes, sizes, and products, including beef muscle, pig ears, smoked hog hide, dehydrated pig snouts, and tightly rolled rawhide. Some colored rawhide chews can stain carpets and furnishings. Cow hooves, while a popular canine favorite, are hard and can chip or break your dog's teeth.

Specially designed rigid nylon and rubber bones and toys are excellent for satisfying your puppy's need to chew.

Rope toys and tugs are often made of 100-percent cotton, and frequently flavored to make them more attractive to your dog. Some have plaque-fighting fluoride floss woven into the rope to deep clean your dog's teeth and gums. Be careful that your puppy cannot shred the cotton ropes, which may be a potential choking hazard.

Teething

Around 4 weeks of age, puppies begin to develop their baby teeth—also known as *deciduous teeth* or *milk teeth*. The process ends when a dog's permanent teeth are in place. Teething varies from puppy to puppy, with most puppies undergoing some form of continuous teething until they are about 6 to 9 months of age. This stimulates an uncontrollable urge to chew as a means of relieving some of the discomfort, and as a way to facilitate the removal of their baby teeth.

Give your puppy plenty of appropriate chew toys while he is teething.

Plush toys vary in their durability. Some are easily shredded by tenacious, seek-and-destroy Aussies who can chew out the squeaky part in record time, while other dogs like to carry them around or snuggle with them. When choosing these toys, opt for the durable models if your puppy is likely to shred, disembowel, and then attempt to consume the innards.

A super-size carrot is often a good chew toy for young puppies. They are tasty, durable, easily digestible, and puppies love them. Stay away from raisins and grapes, which can be toxic in certain quantities.

Digging

Dogs love to dig. It's another fact of dog ownership. Some breeds dig more so than others, and their idea of fun can cause you a significant amount of frustration and heartache, especially when your precious pooch digs his way to China right under your newly planted garden. Generally speaking, Australian Shepherds are not tenacious diggers when compared to, say, Terriers. Aussies are, however, quite capable of wreaking havoc in your yard given the right incentive, such as gophers or a stinky manure pile.

If your Aussie digs, and you don't care that his full-time job is excavating your yard, you have nothing to worry about. Let him dig away, provided, of course, it is safe for him to do so. However, if you prefer not to have potholes in your garden and lawn, prevention is the best solution.

Is He Bored?

Some dogs dig holes to bury their favorite toys or bones. Others dig to find a cool spot to escape the heat. Most dogs dig out of frustration or boredom. If your Aussie is digging out of boredom or to release excess energy, do something that stimulates his mind, burns energy, and tires him out. Use your imagination to come up with fun games. For example, purchase a food-dispensing puzzle that allows him to exercise his brain as he tries to outsmart the toy. Give him chew toys that can be stuffed with squeeze cheese or peanut butter and provide your Australian Shepherd with hours of entertainment. Or, play fun Find It games, where you hide a tasty tidbit of food under a small box or bucket and encourage him to find it. Play hide-and-seek games that encourage him to find you.

Is He Hot?

If your Australian Shepherd is digging to find a cool spot to escape the heat, his digging may be the least of your problems. Like most dogs, Aussies do not tolerate hot weather well. Get him

Teach Your Puppy Right from Wrong

When you supervise your puppy in the house, you are able to monitor his whereabouts and, in the process, provide him with appropriate chew toys. While you are watching television, have one or two chew toys available for your puppy. Encourage him to chew by showing him the toy. When you see him settle down to chew on it, calmly praise him. Then allow him to chew without interruption. You can try tethering him to the leg of the couch or coffee table with a lightweight leash to prevent him from wandering off. Of course, supervision at all times is essential. Otherwise he's likely to chew the table or couch leg.

Until your puppy is reliable, it is never wise to give him free run of the house. Remember, puppies are individuals. It is impossible to arbitrarily put an age on when a puppy is reliably trained. Some puppies have a stronger desire to chew than others. A general guideline is about 1 year of age. Much will depend on how conscientious and committed you are to managing your puppy's environment, instilling good behaviors, and discouraging unwanted behaviors.

As your puppy grows and matures, his desire to chew will diminish. It is important, however, to continue giving him bones and chew toys throughout his life to exercise his jaws, keep his teeth clean, and entertain him for a few hours.

out of the heat and provide him with a cool spot, such as an air-conditioned room or a cool grassy area with plenty of shade.

Prevention

Many dogs are attracted to the smell of chicken and steer manure, and love to dig and roll in fresh soil and newly fertilized gardens. The best solution for digging in gardens is prevention. Do not allow your Australian Shepherd free access to garden areas where he can dig. An alternative is to install a small fence around the garden, or put chicken wire under the soil so that digging becomes less productive and rewarding for the dog. Or, fence off a section of the yard just for him where he can dig and dig to his heart's content.

Jumping Up

Puppies and adult dogs love to jump on people. It's their way of getting close to your face and saying "Hi!" Licking faces is a natural behavior for dogs when they greet each other, and they don't understand that humans frequently take offense. Of course, if you

You may want to designate a spot in your yard where your dog can dig.

Aussies are exuberant and love to jump.

don't mind your dog jumping on you—and some owners don't—then you have nothing to worry about. However, what you think is cute, harmless puppy behavior is far from amusing when your Australian Shepherd weighs 50 pounds and has four muddy feet.

The key is to discourage all occasions of jumping up. If you do not want your adult dog to jump on you, do not allow the behavior when he is a puppy. It is equally unfair to allow him to jump on you but correct him for jumping on visitors, or to allow him to jump on you today but not tomorrow when you are wearing white pants.

With a young puppy, try crouching down as he comes to greet you. As you do this, slip your thumb in his collar under his chin (your thumb should be pointing down toward the ground) and apply gentle pressure so he cannot jump up. Give him praise only when all four feet are on the ground. Your praise should be sincere, but not overly enthusiastic. Otherwise, you are likely to wind him up even more.

Teach him not to jump by making him Sit for a kiss or cookie. Aussies are smart, but even the smartest one hasn't figured out how to simultaneously Sit for a cookie and jump on you.

To prevent your puppy (or adult dog) from jumping on visitors, put his leash on before you open the door. This allows you to control his behavior without grabbing at his fur or collar. When he sits nicely without pawing or mauling your guests, calmly praise and reward him with a tasty tidbit. "That's my good boy!" or "What a good sit!"

Small children like to run, flail their arms, and make loud squealing noises. This type of behavior is especially attractive to young puppies. Most young children cannot control a jumping puppy, let alone a 50-pound Aussie. Therefore, always supervise children, and manage your dog so he is not put in a position where

Good breeders will begin socialization early to help avoid problem behaviors in the future.

he can develop bad habits or inadvertently get himself into trouble.

Running Off or Not Coming when Called

Australian Shepherds who run away from their owners or refuse to come when called can create an enormous amount of frustration and angst for their owners. The good news is that it is one of the easiest problems to solve. The key is to never allow your puppy to develop the bad habit of running off. Do you see a pattern of preventive behavior developing? Each and every time you go outside, your puppy should be on leash. If you want your puppy to run around and explore his surroundings, let him drag his leash or a lightweight long-line. If your puppy starts to wander off, simply step on the long-line and reel him back in.

If your adult dog has already developed the annoying habit of running off or ignoring your Come command, a leash or long-line will prevent him from continuing to do so. Then, go back and re-teach him to Come when called. You also should never get in the habit of chasing your puppy, or allowing your kids to chase your puppy. Dogs think this is a fun game, but it teaches a dog to run away from you, which is not only annoying but dangerous. A puppy or adult dog who runs away from his owner can easily dart into traffic and cause serious injury to himself.

Seeking Professional Help

Despite your best efforts to raise a well-behaved Australian Shepherd, undoubtably times will arise when things go terribly, terribly wrong, and you may need to call in an expert. Some problems, such as aggression and separation anxiety, are difficult and complicated areas of canine behavior that require expert guidance. These behaviors are multifaceted and often have overlapping causes. For example, genetics, lack of socialization, sexual maturity/frustration, lack of obedience training, inappropriate correction, and pain are a few of the reasons why dogs might display aggression. Dogs with true separation anxiety issues can work themselves into a frenzy. They salivate, pace, whine, bark, and work themselves into an uncontrollable state of panic, destroying anything and everything they can get their teeth and paws on, including couches, walls, doors, rugs, and plants.

7

ADVANCED TRAINING AND ACTIVITIES
With Your Australian Shepherd

ustralian Shepherds have a "Send me in, Coach!" attitude, which makes training and showing them a great deal of fun. A truly versatile breed, they are capable of competing in multiple venues, such as agility, herding, obedience, and even Schutzhund. Training and competing with your Aussie is a great way to build a strong and mutually respectful relationship—and have a great deal of fun in the process. Conformation is the cornerstone of the American Kennel Club (AKC), Australian Shepherd Club of America (ASCA), and Kennel Club (KC) shows, but if your Aussie is not breed quality, don't worry, there are lots of activities you can enter that will stimulate your Aussie's mind and allow him to strut his agility, athleticism, and intelligence. Through AKC-sanctioned events alone, you and your Aussie can participate in agility, Canine Good Citizen, conformation, herding, obedience, rally obedience, and tracking.

AGILITY

Agility is one of the fastest growing sports for dogs, and one of the most exciting, fast-paced canine events for spectators. Similar to equestrian Grand Prix courses, canine agility courses include assorted jumps and hurdles. Dogs demonstrate their agile nature and versatility by maneuvering through a timed obstacle course of jumps, tunnels, A-frames, weave poles, ramps, a teeter-totter, and a pause box.

An agility handler navigates her dog through successive obstacles while trying to regulate the dog's speed and precision, and, of course, trying to stay the heck out of the way of a fast-moving Aussie. A perfect score in any class is 100. Competitors are faulted if they go over the allotted course time or receive a penalty, such as taking an obstacle out of sequence, missing a contact zone, touching the dog, and so forth.

All-breed agility trials are the most common. These events are open to all AKC breeds and varieties of dogs. Specialty trials are restricted to dogs of a specific breed or varieties of one breed.

Agility consists of obstacles like jumps and tunnels.

Classes and Titles

As with other canine events, both AKC and ASCA offer similar classes and titles. ASCA began its agility program in 1995, and offers three title classes: Regular Agility, Jumpers, and Gamblers. Three levels are offered within each title class: Novice, Open, and Elite.

AKC trials offer two types of title classes: Standard and Jumpers with Weaves. The Standard class has a pause box and contact obstacles—those yellow contact zones at each end of the obstacle. The dog must place at least one paw in the contact zone or receive a fault. The goal is to encourage safety in training and in running the course. The Jumpers with Weaves class also has a variety of obstacles but does not have contact obstacles or a pause box that slows the competitor's forward momentum. Within each agility class there are different levels of competition:

- **Novice**: For the dog who is just starting in agility. The course features 13 to 15 obstacles, and the focus is on completing each obstacle with a minimum of handling skill required.
- **Open**: For the dog who has completed the Novice level. The course features 16 to 18 obstacles, and the degree of difficulty increases. The Open class also requires significantly more handling skills than does the Novice class.
- **Excellent**: For the dog who has completed the Open level. The course features 18 to 20 obstacles, the degree of difficulty increases significantly, and the focus is on providing competitors with the opportunity to demonstrate

their superior training, communication, and handling skills.

For the die-hard agility competitor, the Master Agility Champion Title (MACH) is the pinnacle of agility competition. To achieve a MACH title, a dog must exhibit speed and consistency on the agility course. He must receive a minimum of 750 champion points and 20 double-qualifying scores from the Excellent B Standard and Excellent B Jumpers and Weaves class. To put it in layman terms, handlers receive one champion point for each full second under the standard course time. They can double the championship points received if they place first in their class. It's challenging, but not impossible for the Aussie owner.

The only drawback to agility is that it requires a lot of equipment, which can be pretty expensive to purchase. If you are handy with a hammer and saw, you can build a lot of the equipment yourself. The best way to get started in agility is to join a local dog-training club or visit an agility training facility.

CANINE FREESTYLE

Canine freestyle is an engaging canine sport that allows you and your Australian Shepherd to kick up your heels, so to speak. In simplest terms, canine freestyle is a choreographed performance between a dog and handler, set to music, which usually has a catchy melody and a good dance beat. Dog and owner wear matching costumes or accessories, which also complement the performance.

Don't let the catchy name fool you, though. Canine freestyle is more than dogs heeling to music. The sport is patterned after Olympic skating, with dogs and handlers performing twists, turns, leg kicks, pivots, and other cool and creative maneuvers. These maneuvers are entwined with basic obedience commands, such as heeling, sits, downs, and fronts. Many advanced competitors teach their dogs to crawl, back up, wave, bow, side step, bounce, rollover, spin, and play dead. Freestyle routines vary dramatically, and are creatively choreographed with an emphasis on the human–canine bond.

Australian Shepherds do very well in this sport because of their natural athleticism, trainability, and their instinct for performing and hamming it up.

As with other canine sports, canine freestyle offers a number of divisions and categories to suit a dog and handler's varying levels of experience. Several organizations promote canine freestyle,

The Origin of Agility

The origin of Agility can be traced across the Atlantic to Great Britain. The sport originated in 1978, as a small-scale demonstration in the main ring at the prestigious Crufts Dog Show. The show committee wanted an entertainment venue to fill the spare time between the Obedience championships and the Group judging. As a result, John Varley and Peter Meanwell designed a challenging obstacle course, borrowing many elements from equestrian events. The challenging obstacles and fast-paced dogs hooked spectators. The rest, as they say, is history.

with styles varying between the organizations. For additional information, contact the Canine Freestyle Federation, Inc. (CFF) or the World Canine Freestyle Organization, Inc. (WCFO).

CANINE GOOD CITIZEN

Training and interacting with your Australian Shepherd is always fun, but if organized competitions are not your cup of tea, the AKC's Canine Good Citizen (CGC) Program might be the perfect alternative. Implemented in 1989, the CGC Program is a public education and certification program designed to promote good dogs and good owners, and to demonstrate that the dog, as a companion to man, can be a respected member of the community. The CGC Program encourages owners to develop a positive and worthwhile relationship with their dogs by rewarding responsible dog ownership and good pet manners. It is designed to encourage owners to get involved with and obedience-train their dogs.

The program does not involve the formality or precision of competitive obedience, but it does lay the foundation for good pet manners and is often used as a stepping stone for other canine activities, such as obedience, rally obedience, and agility.

The CGC program is a noncompetitive, ten-part test that

Canine Good Citizen Program tests your dog's behavior in practical situations.

evaluates your Australian Shepherd's behavior in practical situations at home, in public, and in the presence of unfamiliar people and other dogs. The pass or fail test is designed to test an Australian Shepherd's reaction to distractions, friendly strangers, and supervised isolation. Additionally, an Australian Shepherd must sit politely while being petted, walk on a loose leash, walk through a crowd, and respond to basic obedience commands including Sit, Down, Stay, and Come. The evaluator also inspects the dog to determine if he is clean and groomed. An Aussie who successfully completes the test receives a certificate stating he is a Canine Good Citizen, entitled to use the initials "CGC" behind his name.

CGC tests are offered by local dog-training clubs and are often given in conjunction with dog shows or matches. Humane societies occasionally sponsor CGC tests, too. Both purebred and mixed-breed dogs are eligible to participate. While there is no age limit, dogs must be old enough to have received their immunizations.

CONFORMATION (SHOWING)

Conformation shows (dog shows) are the signature events of the competitive dog world. The conformation ring, commonly referred to as the *breed ring*, provides a forum for breeders and handlers to showcase the best in breeding stock. These animals are evaluated as potential breeding stock, and are usually incorporated into future breeding programs in an effort to improve the breed. For this reason, dogs competing in conformation cannot be spayed or neutered.

How Dog Shows Work

The best way to understand the conformation ring is to think of it in terms of an elimination process. Each Australian Shepherd enters a regular class and is evaluated against the Australian Shepherd breed standard. For the newcomer, it often appears as if the dogs are competing against one another. And, in a sense, they are. However, the judge is not comparing the quality of one Australian Shepherd against the quality of another Australian Shepherd. The judge is evaluating each Australian Shepherd against the breed standard and how closely each dog measures up to the ideal Australian Shepherd as outlined in the breed standard.

The regular classes are divided by sex, with the male and female dogs judged separately. The male dogs are always judged first and, after being examined by the judge, they are placed first through fourth according to how well they measure up to the Australian Shepherd breed standard in the judge's opinion. After the males have been judged, the females go through the same judging process.

After the regular classes have been judged, the first place winners of each class are brought back to the ring to compete against one another in the Winners Class. The dog selected is the Winners Dog and is awarded championship points. A Reserve Winners Dog is also chosen, but does not receive points unless the Winners Dog, for any reason, is disallowed or disqualified. The same process is then repeated with the female dogs, resulting in a Winners Bitch and Reserve Winners Bitch.

The Winners Dog and Winners Bitch go back into the ring with

Benched Shows

Conformation shows are either benched or unbenched. At a benched show, dogs are grouped together by breed in a central area and are on display during the entire show, except for grooming, exercising, and showing. A benched show is an educational venue that allows spectators to view, admire, and learn about dog breeds in an up-close and controlled surrounding. While a few shows remain benched — including the prestigious Westminster Kennel Club show and the U.K.'s prestigious Crufts Dog Show — the majority of shows today are unbenched. Dogs may be kept anywhere when not showing, and you are not required to stay on the show grounds after you show your dog.

Dog shows evaluate how closely a dog comes to matching the breed standard.

any Champions entered to compete for the Best of Breed award. If either the Winners Dog or Winners Bitch wins Best of Breed or Best of Winners, they may also win more points. In AKC shows the Best of Breed dog or bitch then goes on to the Group. The Group winners are then judged with Group placements—first through fourth place—being awarded in each of the seven groups. The first place Group winners compete for the most coveted and most prestigious award: Best in Show.

Earning a Championship

To attain an AKC Championship title, each Australian Shepherd must win a total of 15 points. Only the Winners Dog and Winners Bitch receive points. The number of points earned at each show is predetermined by a point schedule that varies from region to region.

The number of points awarded at each show depends on the breed, the number of dogs entered in the competition, and the location of the show. For example, points awarded to an Australian Shepherd in New York will differ from the number of points awarded in California. The number of points that can be won at a show is between one and five. Three-, four-, and five-point wins are considered *majors*. One- and two-point wins are considered *minors*. Of the 15 points required for a Championship title, six or more of the points must be majors. The remaining points may be attained in any combination, including major or minor wins, but these points must be won under different judges than were the two major wins. So, you need to win points under at least three different judges. An Australian Shepherd can add to the number of points he won in the Winners Class if he also wins Best of Breed, Best of Opposite Sex, or Best of Winners. Once the requirements are met and officially confirmed, then a championship certificate is issued for the individual dog.

Earning an ASCA Title

Earning an ASCA championship title is similar to the requirements for an AKC championship. Both titles require 15 points; however, ASCA requires that 9 of the 15 points be majors. ASCA shows also have Best of Breed, but no Best in Show competition.

Showing Your Australian Shepherd

Dog showing is a gratifying and rewarding way to meet new

people, spend countless hours with your Australian Shepherd, and build a strong human–canine bond. However, dog showing, like most sports, is an art that must be learned and practiced regularly. If you are interested in conformation shows, you must learn to groom, condition, and present your Australian Shepherd in the best possible light. You will need to learn about the structure and movement of Australian Shepherds. You will need to dress appropriately—not so flashy that you detract from your dog, but not so casual that you look like you came straight from mucking stalls. You will need proper shoes that provide comfort and are suitable for running. You'll have no control over many things—the weather, judging schedules, bitches that come into season, schedules that move more slowly than you like—but you can control how you and your dog are represented and presented in the ring.

Regardless of the event, you must have a thorough understanding and comprehension of the rules and regulations governing the show. You should obtain a copy of the rules and regulations for the governing organization (AKC, ASCA, KC, or UKC) and read it thoroughly. Most importantly, you must learn the art of winning and losing. Showing dogs requires a great deal of patience and objectivity. There will always be differences of opinion, shows you thought you should have won, and shows you won that you never should have. You must learn to be humble in your wins and gracious in your defeats.

The best way to get involved in showing dogs is to attend shows

All-Breed, Specialty, and Group Shows

The AKC sponsors three types of conformation shows.

All-breed shows are exactly what the name implies. Open to over 150 breeds and varieties of dogs recognized by the American Kennel Club, these shows include the prestigious Westminster Kennel Club show. These are the conformation shows you are most likely to see on television.

Specialty shows are for one specific breed, such as the Australian Shepherd. Most often, local, regional, or national breed-specific clubs sponsor these shows.

Group shows are limited to dogs belonging to one of the seven groups (Herding, Toy, Sporting, Hound, Terrier, Non-Sporting, and Working),. For example, a Herding group show would feature only breeds belonging to the Herding group.

Show dogs must learn to stand in a "stacked" pose.

If your dog enjoys playing with a Frisbee you might want to try a flying disc competition.

and ask a lot of questions. Most dog people are more than willing to help the newcomer. If possible, join a local dog club and find a mentor, such as an Australian Shepherd breeder or professional handler, who is willing to help you maneuver the ins and outs of dog shows.

FLYBALL

Invented in the late 1970s, flyball is yet another exhilarating choice in the list of entertaining sports you can do with your Australian Shepherd. It's the perfect "game" for all tennis ball-loving Aussies! To say flyball is fast-paced is an understatement. It is a high-octane relay race that showcases your Aussie's speed and agility. Don't worry—your Australian Shepherd does all the running in this game. It is a team sport rather than an individual competition, and an equally thrilling and entertaining spectator sport.

The course consists of four hurdles (small jumps) spaced approximately 10 feet (3 m) apart. Fifteen feet (4 m) beyond the last hurdle is a spring-loaded box that contains a tennis ball. Just as in any relay race, the fastest team to successfully complete the game wins. The goal is for each dog to take a turn running the relay by leaping each of the four hurdles and then hitting a pedal or lever with his paw to trigger the box, which shoots a tennis ball up in the air. Once the dog catches the ball in his mouth, he races back over the four hurdles to the finish line, where the next dog is anxiously awaiting his turn.

The first team to have all four dogs run without errors wins the heat. If a dog misses a hurdle or fails to retrieve the ball, he must repeat his turn. For additional information, contact the North American Flyball Association or the British Flyball Association.

HERDING

Herding is your Aussie's heritage. For more than 100 years, Aussies and Aussie-type dogs have been selectively bred and developed as farm and ranch dogs, as well as "a companion and guardian of the family and the family's possessions." A lot of Aussies are still utilized in a working environment by farmers and ranches around the country. However, a good number of Aussies are full-time pets and live in the city and suburbs—far removed from the sights, smells, and activities of livestock or a working environment. The good news is that you and your Aussie—even if he is a city slicker—can still get involved and compete in recreational or competitive herding.

Sheepdog trials in the United States are fashioned after British trials, and are considered a true test of sheepdog skills. They are designed to parallel the everyday work of a sheepdog in a working environment and, while each trial is a bit different, they normally consist of an outrun, lift, fetch, drive, pen, and shed. Sheepdog trials welcome any herding breed, but they are more closely associated with Border Collies, who dominate the trials. Australian Shepherds can and do occasionally compete in them, but you are more likely to find Aussies strutting their stuff at ASCA-sanctioned stockdog trials or AKC herding trials.

ASCA's Stockdog Program

The primary function of ASCA's stockdog program is to preserve and promote the breed's natural herding instinct and its original function as a versatile stockdog. Trials provide a competitive venue for owners and dogs to showcase their working skill and handling talent. Trials help to establish better breeding and training programs

Catch a Flying Disc!

The Australian Shepherd's athleticism, speed, trainability, and natural desire to retrieve fast moving objects make him the perfect Frisbee or flying disc competitor. No doubt you have seen these high-flying, talented Aussies competing on televised programs, such as Animal Planet or ESPN's Great Outdoor Games.

Several organizations sponsor flying disc competitions including Skyhoundz, Unified Frisbee Dog Operations, and International Disc Dog Handlers' Association.

Herding is part of your Aussie's heritage.

because they encourage a high standard of performance in Aussies and all herding dogs. Equally important, they provide owners with an opportunity to study good working dogs and evaluate the qualities most desired.

ASCA offers stockdog titles in three levels of training on three classes of stock: cattle (c), sheep (s), or ducks (d). Each level is divided into classes:

- **Started**: The first level of competition for dogs who are 6 months of age or older, and who have not yet earned a certification in the stock class being entered, be it cattle, sheep, or ducks. Aussies who receive two qualifying scores (69 points out of a possible 100) from two different judges earn the Started Trial Dog (STD) certification.
- **Open**: The next level for dogs who have earned an STD certification for the stock class entered. Dogs who receive two qualifying scores (88 points out of a possible 125, and at least 40 percent of the course score) from two different judges receives the Open Trial Dog (OTD) certification.
- **Advanced**: The final level, for dogs who have earned an OTD certification for the stock class entered. As with the STD and OTD classes, a dog who earns two qualifying scores (88 points out of a possible 125 and at least 50 percent of the total course score) under two different judges earns the Advanced Trial Dog (ATD) certification.

Your Aussie does not need to earn certification on all classes of livestock. For example, he does not need to earn an STD on sheep, cattle, and ducks before moving up to the Open division. However, the class certifications must be earned in order: Started, Open, Advanced. So, if he earns his Started Certification in the sheep class (STDs), he must then earn his Open Certification (OTDs) before moving up to the Advanced Certification (ATDs). The same process is followed for each division of livestock.

In addition to the above classes, ASCA offers a Working Trial Championship (WTCH) title. A WTCH is the crème de la crème of herding, because dogs must earn two qualifying scores under two different judges at each level and on each class of stock.

AKC Herding Tests

As Australian Shepherds become increasingly popular as pets, many owners are dabbling in AKC-sponsored events designed to test their dog's herding instinct. These tests and trials are artificial simulations of working pastoral or farm conditions, but they are not always reflective of true farm work. However, they do provide a standardized test by which owners can measure their dog's inherent herding abilities and training.

The AKC herding program has two major divisions: Herding Tests and Herding Trials.

Herding Tests are non-competitive tests intended for dogs with minimum herding experience. Dogs must, however, show a sustained interest in herding livestock. Within this division, owners can earn two certifications: HT (Herding Tested Dog), which indicates a dog has shown herding instinct and is under basic control, and a PT (Pre-trial Tested Dog), which indicates that a dog and handler worked together as a team. Dogs must possess a modest amount of training, but are not yet skilled enough to compete in the lowest level trial. A pre-trial test helps novice handlers develop the skills necessary to compete successfully at trial level.

Herding Trials are competitive trials intended for dogs with substantial training.

Herding Trials are competitive trials intended for dogs with substantial training. Dogs must demonstrate the ability to move and control livestock. The titles awarded in each division are: Herding Started (HS), Herding Intermediate (HI), Herding Advanced (HX).

Unlike ASCA's stockdog program, AKC titles

need not be earned in order; however, once your Aussie earns a qualifying score in an upper class, he can't go back to a lower class on that course/stock.

When an Aussie has completed his HX title, he is eligible to compete for a Herding Champion Certificate (HC). A Herding Champion dog must have earned an HX and at least 15 championship points in the advanced classes.

OBEDIENCE

Every aspect of dog ownership involves some form of obedience training, yet the obedience ring seldom, if ever, receives the PR and media attention of other canine events. An obedience competition goes well beyond the CGC Program and tests an Australian Shepherd's ability to perform a prescribed set of exercises in a formal environment. Some compare it to ballroom dancing, because both dog and owner are extensions of each other—both working in sync. Others compare it to the formal and elegant equine dressage

tests, with owners achieving a harmonious relationship with their dogs, all the while observing meticulous attention to minute details.

In addition to enriching the bond and relationship between a dog and handler, obedience training is designed to emphasize "the usefulness of purebred dogs as the ultimate companion and helpmate to man, and as a means of recognizing that dogs have been trained to behave in the home, in public places, and in the presence of other dogs."

Both the AKC and ASCA offer obedience titles. Rules, regulations, and requirements vary slightly between the two organizations. However, the primary requirements for earning titles are basically the same.

Obedience Tip

The best way to get involved in obedience is to sign up for a dog obedience class or join a local dog obedience club. If you are interested in competitive obedience, it is helpful to find a trainer who successfully competes in the sport and teaches competitive obedience classes.

There are three levels of competitive obedience:

- **The Novice Level**: The dog is required to heel on and off leash at a normal, fast, and slow pace; come when called; stand for a physical examination by the judge; and do a sit-stay and a down-stay with other dogs. Other than giving commands, handlers are not allowed to talk to their dog during the exercise, nor are they allowed to use toys, treats, or other training aids in the ring. Dogs who complete this level receive a Companion Dog (CD) title.

- **The Open Level**: The Open class is quite a bit more difficult than the Novice class because all exercises are performed off leash. A dog will be required to do similar heelwork exercises as in the Novice class, as well as a retrieve exercise, a drop on recall, a high jump, broad jump, and a sit-stay and a down-stay with other dogs while the handlers are out of sight. Dogs who complete this level receive a Companion Dog Excellent (CDX) title.

- **The Utility Level**: Utility is the final and most difficult and challenging level of training. The exercises include scent discrimination, directed jumping, retrieving, hand signals, and a moving stand and examination. Completing this level awards your dog a Utility Dog (UD) title.

If you've gotten this far, you are seriously committed to the sport of obedience, and you may decide to work toward a Utility Dog Excellent (UDX) or Obedience Trial Championship title (OTCH)—the crème de la crème of obedience competition. While it is considered the most prestigious title, it has also proven to be the most elusive crown since its inception in 1977.

RALLY OBEDIENCE

Rally obedience is the newest AKC event. It is a combination of agility and obedience. However, the emphasis is less on speed and precision and more on how well dogs and handlers perform together as a team. It was created with the average dog owner in mind and as a means to help promote a positive human–canine relationship with an emphasis on fun and excitement. It also takes the pressure off competing, while still allowing owners to showcase their Australian Shepherds' obedience skills.

In rally obedience, the dog and handler move through a course designed by the rally judge. The dog and handler proceed at their own pace through the designated stations—between10 and 20 stations, depending on the level. Each of these stations has a sign providing instructions regarding the skill to be performed, such as Halt & Sit; Halt, Sit, & Down; Right Turn; About Right Turn; or While Heeling Perform a 270-Degree Left Turn.

Unlike traditional obedience competitions, handlers are permitted to talk to their dog, use praise, clap their hands, pat their legs, or use any verbal means of communication and body language throughout the performance. Handlers may not touch their dog or make physical corrections. Any dog who is eligible for AKC registration can enter Rally obedience.

SWIMMING

Swimming is the perfect Rx for cooling off, burning calories, and sharing quality time with your Australian Shepherd. Believe it or not—not all Aussies will take to the water like, well, a fish to water. You may need to take it slowly and introduce your Aussie to water playfully and gradually. Never toss your Aussie into the water. This is neither fair nor humane. Doing so will no doubt frighten him—not to mention possibly injure him and turn him off to swimming and water activities for the rest of his life.

For the reluctant Australian Shepherd, try to find a swimming pool, lake, or shallow pond that has a gentle sloping bank. Kiddy pools or wading pools are also excellent for the hesitant swimmer. Encourage your Aussie to wade in with you or throw a floatable toy for him to retrieve, being careful in the beginning to toss it close to the bank of the pond or edge of the pool. If you toss it too far, it is likely he will find the task of retrieving too daunting.

Nothing beats an invigorating walk on the beach with your Aussie. Your dog may be content to dip his feet in the foam, or he may be more adventurous and take a full-body plunge. It is important to keep your Aussie close to shore regardless of his superior athleticism and swimming capabilities. Riptides and undercurrents are unpredictable, and your Aussie can quickly wade into trouble.

Most Aussies will play until they exhaust themselves, collapsing into a heap of sleep.

Therefore, always watch for signs that your Aussie is getting tired, such as panting, slowing down, or slapping the water with his front feet. A lifejacket designed specifically for dogs may provide a safety net for your water-loving companion.

TRACKING

Tracking is a popular sport that tests an Australian Shepherd's ability to recognize and track a human scent over varying terrains and climatic changes. It is designed to showcase a dog's intelligence and extremely high level of scent capability, which should be pretty easy for an Aussie, right?

Teach your Aussie to track for fun, such as finding his toys or a treat you've hidden in the house or around the yard. Teach him to "Go find the kids" or find a wayward senior dog. Or teach him to track as a sport.

Titles

Both the AKC and ASCA offer tracking titles. The AKC offers three tracking titles: Tracking Dog (TD), Tracking Dog Excellent (TDX), and Variable Surface Tracking (VST). If an Australian

Sports and Safety

Before beginning any physically challenging activity with your Australian Shepherd, take him to the veterinarian's for a thorough check-up and examination. Joint problems, such as hip and elbow dysplasia, show up in some Australian Shepherds and should be of paramount concern for owners. They may preclude your Aussie from some of the more physically demanding activities. Low-stress activities are wonderful for puppies, but young dogs (generally under the age of 2 years) should never be allowed to jump. Too much pressure on developing joints and limbs can injure your puppy and lead to lifelong problems. No one wants that.

Shepherd successfully completes all three tracking titles, he earns the prestigious title of Champion Tracker (CT). ASCA offers two titles: Tracking Dog (TD) and Tracking Dog Excellent (TDX).

The rules and regulations vary slightly for each organization. However, the primary goal is for the dog to follow a scented track and locate an article left at the end of the trail by a tracklayer.

For an Australian Shepherd to earn an AKC TD title, the dog must follow a track laid by a human tracklayer. The track must be 440 to 500 yards (402 to 457 m) with three to five changes of direction, and the track must be *aged* at least 30 minutes but not more than 2 hours before the dog can begin scenting (following the track).

A TDX title is the next level, and it is slightly more difficult than a TD. It is earned when an Australian Shepherd follows a track that is between 800 and 1,000 yards (732 to 914 m) and between 3 and 5 hours old. The TDX track must have five to seven directional changes and also include the additional challenge of human cross tracks, which, as the name implies, is a human track that crosses the primary track. A dog must also locate four articles, rather than the one article required for a TD.

TD and TDX tracks are laid through open fields and wilderness

You can come up with your own fun sport to do with your Aussie.

areas and include varying terrain conditions, such as gullies, plowed land, woods, and vegetation. However, urban sprawl has severely limited those spaces in some parts of the country. As a result, the Variable Surface Tracking (VST) title was designed to utilize industrial and office parks, college campuses, and so forth. To earn a VST title, dogs must first have a TD title, and they must follow a track that is 600 to 800 yards (547 to 732 m) in length and between 3 to 5 hours old. The track may take them down a street, between buildings, across a college campus, asphalt parking lot, concrete sidewalk, and the like.

Unlike obedience and agility titles that require a dog and handler to qualify three times, an Australian Shepherd only needs to complete one track successfully to earn each title. If you and your Australian Shepherd love the great outdoors—tracking might be the sport for you. The best way to get involved in tracking is to contact a local dog obedience club or a national organization, such as the United States Australian Shepherd Association, Australian Shepherd Club of America, American Kennel Club, The Kennel Club, or Canadian Kennel Club.

WALKING, JOGGING, HIKING

The Australian Shepherd is a natural trotter and, if built correctly and conditioned properly, he can trot for long distances. As a result, Aussies make excellent exercise companions and, no doubt, you and your Aussie will benefit from the cardiovascular workout and companionship. It is worth reiterating that Australian Shepherds can and do suffer from heat-induced illnesses. Therefore, if you plan to include your Australian Shepherd in your daily walks or jogs, limit these activities to cooler parts of the day, such as the early morning or evening. Equally important, hot sidewalks and roads can burn an Aussie's feet, causing an enormous amount of pain and discomfort. If the sidewalks and roadways are too hot for your bare feet, chances are they will be too hot for your Aussie's paws. How far your Aussie can walk, jog, or hike, will depend on his age, physical condition, the terrain covered, and the weather. An extended hike through rough terrain and rocky surfaces may be a piece of

Enjoy Winter Sports? Try Skijoring!

In its simplest terms, skijoring is being pulled on skis by one or more dogs in harness. The great thing about skijoring is almost any dog (over 30 pounds) can participate, which makes it ideal for your sporty, athletic Australian Shepherd. With a minimum amount of equipment, an eager Aussie, and a pair of cross-country skis, you can have the time of your life — while building a strong human–canine bond.

Skijoring is fairly easy to learn, but it does require some basic skills. You should be somewhat proficient on cross-country skis, your Australian Shepherd must be accustomed to wearing a harness, and he must know how to pull, which usually isn't a problem for Aussies! Your Aussie should know some basic obedience skills, as well. It's fun, it's exhilarating, and it's the perfect canine sport if you and your Aussie enjoy winter sports and the great outdoors.

cake for the conditioned dogs, but too taxing for some canine couch potatoes. Carry plenty of fluid for both you and your Australian Shepherd.

CANINE CAREERS

Herding is your Aussie's ancestry, but the breed has been known to excel in assistance and therapy work, too.

A well-trained, socialized Aussie can make a great therapy dog.

Assistance Dogs/Service Dogs

The terms *therapy dogs* and *service dogs* are often used interchangeably. However, there is a significant difference. The Americans with Disabilities Act (ADA) uses the term *service dog* to define a dog who has been "individually trained to work or perform tasks for the benefit of a person with a disability." Professionals within the industry often refer to them as *assistance dogs*, rather than service dogs. *Therapy dogs* provide companionship and emotional support, but do not perform tasks, and federal law does not legally define them.

Under the umbrella of assistance dogs there are four categories: therapy dogs, guide dogs, service dogs, and hearing dogs. While Aussies do serve quite respectfully as guide dogs for the blind, hearing-alert dogs for the hearing impaired, and service dogs for the disabled, organizations tend to employ Golden Retrievers, Labrador Retrievers, or German Shepherds for those jobs. You are most likely to see Aussies doing therapy work.

Therapy Dogs

Therapy is an important area in which Australian Shepherds can help enhance the human–canine bond by providing unconditional love, companionship, and emotional support to nursing home, hospital, assisted living, and mental health residents. Owners volunteering with their Australian Shepherds make regularly scheduled visits and brighten the lives of residents by providing stimulation, companionship, and a vehicle for conversation and interaction.

Only Australian Shepherds who are well mannered and have a sound temperament should undertake this work. While it is personally satisfying to see how your Aussie can brighten the lives of residents, 90 percent of the work is done by your dog, and he must have the physical and mental fortitude to cope with strange noises and smells, distractions, and often erratic behaviors. Additionally, your Aussie must be willing to accept a considerable amount of attention, petting, and touching from strangers. It helps if your dog has a foundation of basic obedience training or his CGC certificate. While the AKC does offer CGC certifications, they do not certify therapy dogs.

Weight Pull

Canine weight-pull competitions are not unlike tractor-pull competitions — except your Aussie is doing all the work! Dogs compete within their individual weight class to see which dog can pull the most weight over 16 feet (4.8 m). A dog can pull a weighted sled on snow or a wheeled cart on a natural surface, and the weight is gradually increased until one dog remains.

Dogs wear specially designed harnesses that disperse tension and reduce the possibility of injury. It's worth mentioning that dogs excel at this venue because they love to work — not because they are being forced to pull. As with all canine activities, start slowly and progress at a rate suitable for the mental and physical capabilities of your dog. Dogs must be 2 years old to compete in weight pulls sanctioned by the International Weight Pulling Association, but they can begin light training around 18 months of age.

While the AKC does not sanction weight-pulling competitions, titles are available through a number of dog clubs and organizations including the United Kennel Club and the International Weight Pull Association (IWPA).

8

HEALTH

of Your Australian Shepherd

s an Aussie owner, one of your most important responsibilities—in addition to training, grooming, and providing quality nutrition—is providing good and regular veterinary care for your dog. Few Aussies—despite being well cared for—are lucky enough to live their entire lives without an illness or injury, and any number of inherited or infectious diseases, parasites, injuries, and serious ailments can jeopardize your Australian Shepherd's good health. The good news is that today's top-notch veterinarians have the training and expertise to help prevent and reduce serious illness. Of course, veterinary services are not cheap either—especially if you see a specialist, such as a canine cardiologist or ophthalmologist, so you might want to consider some form of canine health insurance.

CHOOSING THE RIGHT VETERINARIAN

It is never too early to begin looking for a veterinarian. If your new Aussie has yet to arrive at your home, or you have recently moved, find a veterinarian before you actually need one. It's never a good idea to be scanning the Yellow Pages when your Aussie is sick or injured. Just as you spent a great deal of time and energy finding the right Australian Shepherd , invest time and energy in finding a suitable veterinarian with whom you and your four-legged friend will feel comfortable and can build a mutually trusting and respectful relationship.

Finding the right vet is not difficult, but it may take some time and a bit of detective work. The good news is the hard work you invest today will pay off in the future when you need to put your Australian Shepherd's health and well being in the hands of a veterinarian.

To start your search:
- Ask your Aussie's breeder for a referral. Most reputable breeders know several local veterinarians and specialists.
- Ask friends, family, neighbors, and colleagues who own a pet for a referral.
- Ask around at local dog clubs, obedience schools, dog groomers, or

boarding kennels. These people are usually involved in dogs and will have established a relationship with one or more local veterinarians.

- Local telephone directories are a good starting point. They will give you the names, addresses, and telephone numbers of veterinary and emergency clinics in your area.

THE CLINIC

Visiting clinics can be a time-consuming, but time invested today will be well worth the effort down the road. When visiting veterinary clinics, don't be afraid to ask for a tour of their exam rooms, x-ray room, operating and recovery rooms, boarding areas, and so forth. If the clinic is busy or an emergency arises, you may need to schedule an appointment, which is not an unreasonable request. If the staff or veterinarians refuse to show you their facilities, run, don't walk, to the nearest exit.

Don't be afraid to ask questions when visiting a clinic—it's the best way to find a place where you will be comfortable and confident taking your Aussie. Ask about their regular office hours, holiday and weekend hours, and how emergencies are handled. What type of services do they offer (surgeries, hip or elbow x-rays, ultrasound, dentistry, eye exams, endoscopy), and is the veterinarian familiar with the Aussie breed?

Find a veterinarian before you bring your puppy home.

What to Look For in Clinics

Keep your eye out for these issues:

- The clinic should be neat and clean.
- Exam rooms should be cleaned and disinfected between animals.
- The clinic should be organized and run smoothly; a noisy and chaotic place might not be your best bet.
- A fenced or grassy area should be provided for your Aussie to relieve himself.
- The waiting area should provide adequate room for separating large and small dogs, unruly dogs from nervous dogs, and rambunctious dogs from shy dogs.

PREVENTIVE CARE

Once you have found a good veterinarian, it is time to get your Aussie an appointment. Generally speaking, you should get your new pooch to the veterinarian within 48 to 72 hours after acquiring him. This establishes a record of health. A puppy or adult dog who, to the untrained eye, appears healthy can still have a serious problem. As a new Aussie owner, it is important to work with your veterinarian to develop a preventive healthcare plan and schedule routine visits.

The First Exam

Your veterinarian will check your Aussie's overall condition, including inspecting his skin, coat, eyes, ears, feet, lymph nodes, glands, teeth, and gums. He will listen to his heart and lungs; feel his abdomen, muscles, and joints; and take his temperature. He will ask you about your puppy's daily routine, his eating and elimination habits, and so forth. It is a good idea to jot down any relevant information beforehand so you have it at your fingertips, such as the type of food your puppy eats; how much and how often he eats and drinks; how often he relieves himself; and the color, shape and size of his stools. The veterinarian also should discuss a preventive health care plan that includes vaccinations, worming, spaying or neutering, and the importance of scheduling routine veterinary visits.

Annual Check-Ups

You may not feel older from one birthday to the next, but 1 year is a long time in your Aussie's life. In a relatively short period, about 10 to 12 years, your Aussie will have grown from a tiny puppy to a

The Clinic's Staff

Like human doctors, veterinarians differ in their bedside manners. Some are very personable, caring, and compassionate. Others are less so. Remember, your Aussie's life expectancy is 12 to 15 years, and a good relationship between you and your veterinarian will see you through those years. Otherwise, you will not be comfortable taking your Aussie there, and he will sense your anxiety.

You should be comfortable talking with the veterinarian and asking questions, and you should never feel rushed. He and his staff should be patient, knowledgeable, and friendly, and they should treat your Aussie with kindness, respect, and concern. They should be willing to explain the diagnosis, treatment, and expected outcome in layman's terms.

Of course, there is always the chance that your personality will differ or clash with a particular veterinarian despite, her glowing recommendations and academic qualifications. If this is the case, keep looking until you find the vet who is right for you.

Annual check ups will help keep your adult healthy.

Preparing for Emergencies

Anyone who has ever owned a dog knows that emergencies never happen between 8 a.m. and 5 p.m. It's Murphy's Law with a twist. Anything that can go wrong will go wrong, and it will happen on weekends, holidays, and always after your veterinarian's office has just closed for the day. Therefore, it is always prudent to know the location of the emergency veterinary clinic closest to you. Emergency animal clinics handle emergencies that occur outside of your veterinarian's regular office hours. Most generally, they do not handle routine check-ups, vaccinations, or spaying and neutering.

senior citizen. Experts say 1 human year can be equivalent to 7 to 10 dog years and, in dog circles, that means a lot can happen to your Aussie in the span of 1 year. Some veterinarians recommend bi-annual check-ups—especially for dogs over 7 years of age. This may seem excessive, but remember in 6 short months your Aussie will have aged the equivalent of about 3 to 5 human years.

Aging is an inevitable process, and it's not unusual for owners to inadvertently overlook their Aussie's health. Let's face it: How often do you see your doctor unless you are feeling ill? When your Aussie is happy, healthy, and full of zest, it is easy for annual check-ups to get overlooked. However, it is important to schedule (and keep!) those yearly exams because diseases such as diabetes, kidney failure, arthritis, dental disease, and cancer become more prevalent as your Aussie ages. Older dogs are also more likely to develop problems with their hearing, smell, and sight—not to mention a potpourri of aches, pains, and stiff joints. Yearly check-ups make it more likely that your veterinarian will diagnosis, treat, and perhaps prevent problems early on, before they become major stumbling blocks.

SPAYING AND NEUTERING

A lot of owners have an aversion to spaying or neutering their Australian Shepherd. Rest assured, your dog will not care one iota that he is neutered. He won't get fat—unless you let him. He won't hate you. He won't hold a grudge. He won't be less of a companion, and, contrary to public opinion, he won't even know his "parts" are missing. Females will not make better pets simply because they have been allowed to whelp "just one litter." In fact, quite the opposite is true. Spaying a female and neutering a male prevent unwanted pregnancies that contribute to pet overpopulation. It helps your Aussie to live a longer and healthier life by reducing the incidence of many cancers. Spaying helps to reduce or eliminate breast cancer—especially if a female is spayed before her first heat cycle. It eliminates the incidence of ovarian and uterine infection, and prevents mammary gland tumors—the most common tumor in unsprayed females. In males, neutering eliminates testicular cancer and decreases the incidence of prostate disease.(More than 80 percent of unneutered dogs develop prostate disease.) Neutering also helps to prevent behavioral problems, such as aggression, roaming, and territorial marking (peeing on anything and everything!).

Pros of Spaying and Neutering

- Reduces unwanted pet population
- Reduces incidence of certain cancers
- Helps prevent behavioral problems

While the majority of dogs are altered around 6 months of age, many veterinarians alter dogs as young as 8 weeks of age. Once considered controversial, early spay / neuter procedures are becoming more common. Your veterinarian is the best person to advise you on what age to alter your dog.

VACCINATIONS

Vaccinations are really important for your Aussie puppy. He must be properly socialized starting at a young age, and the sooner he starts his course of vaccinations, the sooner he will be able to get out and about and begin socializing with people and other animals and exploring his new world. A reputable breeder will most likely have administered a series of vaccinations for distemper, hepatitis, leptospirosis, parvovirus, and parainfluenza prior to you acquiring your Aussie. Vaccinations generally start being administered at 6 to 8 weeks of age and continue every 3 to 4 weeks until the puppy is 16 weeks old. You should have received a copy of his vaccination and deworming schedule when you acquired your puppy. It is a good idea to take a copy of your puppy's vaccination schedule with you on your first visit to the veterinarian. Your veterinarian will set up a continued vaccination schedule for your Australian Shepherd depending on where you live, travel plans, and whether your dog has any underlying diseases, such as immune problems or existing infections. Veterinarians differ on their vaccination protocol, but they should be willing to answer your questions and explain the whys and why nots of their practice.

The Vaccination Controversy

Vaccination procedures have been under fire for quite some time, and countless articles have been written on the topic. Decoding the scientific lingo can, unfortunately, be excruciatingly boring, and more than a few people have gone cross-eyed in an attempt to do so. Here are the basics: The majority of experts agree that vaccinations are an important part of canine preventive medicine. They are also in agreement when it comes to puppy vaccinations, and the need to continue vaccinating all dogs for rabies.

Veterinarians used to vaccinate dogs on an annual basis. However, modern science and technology have helped to improve the quality and duration of immunity for many vaccines. Therein lies the controversy. Some experts believe vaccinating dogs on a yearly basis is no longer necessary because of the increased immunity. Many unanswered questions remain regarding the long-term health risks associated with vaccinations. There are also questions regarding the necessity of vaccinating for Lyme disease, Giardia, or even rattlesnake bites. As a result, some researchers advocate rotating yearly vaccines using a single component vaccine—a vaccine, for example, that contains only parvovirus rather than combination vaccines that contain parvovirus, distemper, and hepatitis. An Australian Shepherd could, for example, receive a vaccination for disease "A" one year, and a vaccination for disease "B" the following year. Other veterinarians recommend giving the vaccinations together, but only every 3 years.

There's no question that some vaccinations are an absolute necessity. However, the controversy surrounding vaccinations is not likely to fade anytime too soon. That's why it is important to know the options and discuss vaccination protocol with your veterinarian.

Vaccinations have saved the lives of millions of dogs.

Diseases to Vaccinate Against

The following is a list of viral and bacterial diseases that your veterinarian may recommend vaccinating against—taking into account your lifestyle and where you live.

Coronavirus

Spread through the stool of infected dogs, Coronavirus is highly contagious. Rarely fatal to adult dogs but frequently fatal to puppies, symptoms include vomiting, loss of appetite, and diarrhea, which may lead to dehydration, further endangering puppies. Puppies younger than 12 weeks of age are at the greatest risk. Laboratory tests are necessary to differentiate it from the deadly canine parvovirus.

Discuss a vaccination protocol with your veterinarian.

Distemper

A highly contagious viral disease that is similar to the virus that causes measles in humans, distemper is a primary cause of illness and death in unvaccinated puppies. Spread through the air as well as through contact with an infected animal's stool, distemper spreads rapidly through kennels or multiple-dog households, especially if unvaccinated dogs are present. Distemper attacks a wide range of canine organs including the skin, brain, eyes, respiratory, digestive, and nervous systems. Puppies younger than 6 months of age are in the highest risk bracket. Symptoms may include nasal and eye discharge, coughing, diarrhea, vomiting, and seizures.

Hepatitis

Also known as canine adenovirus, infectious canine hepatitis typically affects the liver, tonsils, and larynx, but can also attack other organs in the body. Spread primarily through infected fluids including saliva, nasal discharge, and urine, symptoms include a sore throat, coughing, and occasionally pneumonia. As it enters an Aussie's bloodstream, it can affect his liver, kidneys, and the appearance of his eyes, which may become cloudy or bluish. More advanced symptoms are characterized by seizures, increased thirst, vomiting, and diarrhea. Unvaccinated Australian Shepherds of all ages are at risk. However, the disease is most prevalent in dogs younger than 1 year of age.

Leptospirosis

A bacterial disease that is transmitted primarily through the urine of infected animals, it can get into water or soil and survive

Also known as canine infectious *tracheobronchitis* or *bordetellosis*, kennel cough is highly contagious and normally characterized by a harsh, dry coughing or hacking, which may be followed by retching and gagging. The disease is airborne—meaning it is passed through the air—and it can spread rapidly among dogs who live together. Dogs at shows, boarding kennels, grooming shops, veterinary clinics, and public or private dog parks are at an increased risk to exposure.

for weeks to months. Australian Shepherds, as well as humans, can become infected through contact with the contaminated urine or the contaminated water or soil. A dog who drinks, swims in, or walks through contaminated water can also become infected. Symptoms can include fever, vomiting, abdominal pain, diarrhea, loss of appetite, weakness, lethargy, stiffness, severe muscle pain, and even death.

Lyme Disease

Caused by the microorganism *Borrelia burgdorferi,* Lyme disease is a bacterial infection that spreads to humans and dogs through the bite of an infected deer tick, also known as the black-legged tick. If infection occurs, the spirochetes migrate, invade, and penetrate into connective tissues, skin joints, and the nervous system, causing arthritis-type symptoms. However, symptoms may not show up for months after initial exposure to an infected tick. Severity of the disease may vary depending on the dog's age and immune status. Symptoms include fever, shifting leg lameness, swelling in the joints, large lymph nodes, and lethargy. Vaccines are available, but their protection is not absolute.

Parvovirus

Spread through the stools of infected dogs, parvovirus is a leading viral cause of diarrhea, and a terrible killer of puppies. This highly contagious gastrointestinal disease normally affects puppies more frequently than adult dogs, with the most severe cases seen in puppies younger than 12 weeks of age. Primary symptoms include an odorous diarrhea, oftentimes dark and bloody. Aussies can be infected with both parvo and coronavirus at the same time, leading to vomiting, dehydration and, in severe cases, lowered white blood cell counts. Healthy adult Aussies generally survive, however the loss of fluids in puppies and older dogs can lead to rapid dehydration, followed by death within a few hours. Time is of the essence. Seek veterinary attention immediately if you suspect your dog has been exposed or shows symptoms, including vomiting or diarrhea.

Rabies

A highly infectious viral disease that affects the brain, rabies is almost invariably fatal once symptoms begin to appear. All warm-blooded animals—including humans—are at risk. Transmission of the virus is almost always from a bite from a rabid animal, such as a bat, raccoon, or skunk. The virus is relatively slow moving, with the average incubation time from exposure to brain involvement (in dogs) being between 2 weeks to 6 months. Behavior changes are frequently the first symptom, and infected dogs have trouble swallowing and will drool or salivate. Advanced symptoms include paralysis and convulsions. Always err on the side of caution and seek veterinary assistance immediately if you suspect a wild animal or an infected dog or cat has bitten your Aussie. Although incurable, properly vaccinated animals are at a relatively low risk of contracting the disease.

HEALTH ISSUES IN THE AUSTRALIAN SHEPHERD

Australian Shepherds, in general, are a pretty healthy breed, with an average lifespan of between 12 and 15 years. Like most breeds, the Australian Shepherd is not immune to health problems. Your Aussie's life will be shaped, influenced, and prolonged by the excellent health care and daily companionship you provide. Unfortunately, however, regardless of your best efforts, your Aussie may develop a health problem. Just as you are a reflection of your parents' genetic contributions, your Aussie is the sum of his genetic makeup, primarily from his parents and grandparents. These genes lay the foundation for his size, markings, structure, temperament, and work ethic, and they will dictate his overall health. This makes acquiring your Aussie from a reputable and knowledgeable breeder doubly important.

Aussies are generally a healthy breed.

Good health starts with good breeding.

The health problems of primary concern to Aussie breeders and owners include allergies, autoimmune diseases, dental faults, epilepsy, eye problems (primarily cataracts and iris coloboma), and hip dysplasia. These health issues are not uncommon in Aussies, but that's not to say your Aussie is going to develop any of these problems. Your Aussie will hopefully live a long, healthy, and problem-free life.

It is worth mentioning that the following information should be used as a guide only, and not as an alternative to treatment by a veterinary practitioner.

Atopic Dermatitis (AD)

Atopic dermatitis is an allergic skin condition caused by a hypersensitivity to environmental allergens that usually include tree, grass, and weed pollens, dust mites, and mold spores—all of which are lightweight and move freely and easily through the air. Exposure to these allergens triggers an immune system response, causing itchy, inflamed skin and sending your Aussie into a vicious cycle of chewing, scratching, digging, and even biting at his skin.

AD normally occurs during the summer and fall, when pollen activity is high. The age of onset is usually between 1 and 3 years of age. However, some dogs may show symptoms as early as 6 months of age. Diagnosis is based on the dog's history (age, sex, breed, affected areas of the body), clinical symptoms (itching, scratching), and ruling out any other conditions that have overlapping symptoms, such as food allergies, parasites, and mange. Although incurable,

AD can usually be controlled using multifaceted treatments, such as immunotherapy, drug therapy, and desensitization. A veterinarian may also prescribe corticosteroids for itching. Reducing your Aussie's exposure to triggering allergens, combined with the use of household air filters, hypoallergenic shampoos, topical anti-itch creams, and omega-3 and omega-6 supplements can help when combined with medical treatment.

Autoimmune Disease

Your Aussie's immune system is like a border patrol, guarding his body against invaders. When the border patrol recognizes an "invader" as foreign or "nonself," such as bacteria, viruses, or parasites, your Aussie's immune system reacts by producing antibodies or sensitized lymphocytes (a type of white blood cell) that seek and destroy the intruders. In normal circumstances, your dog's body recognizes his own tissues and organs as "self" and leaves them alone. In some instances, a dog's immune system short-circuits and begins misidentifying the body's "self" markers as "nonself." When this happens, your Aussie's system mounts an immunological attack against his own tissues or organs.

Several theories exist as to why a dog's immune system short-circuits, but the evidence is empirical rather than scientific. Experts believe there are four main causative factors: genetic predisposition, hormonal influences (especially of sex hormones), infections (especially of viruses), and stress. Other possible triggers include modified live vaccines, ethoxyquin (an antioxidant widely used to preserve fat, vitamin E, and other nutrients in dog food), and antigens, such as beef. All kinds of things act as triggers, so you cannot simply point to a vaccine or a preservative and blame it. Generally speaking, you have a genetically susceptible dog, but something triggers his body, tweaks it into producing abnormal antibodies, and causes an autoimmune problem. The most common autoimmune diseases encountered in Aussies include:

- **Systemic Lupus Erythematosus (SLE).** An autoimmune disease in which a dog's immune system forms antibodies against the nuclear components of its own cells, affecting multiple body systems including joints, kidneys, muscles, and the nervous system, causing arthritis, kidney disease, skin disease, and blood disorders. Symptoms include shifting lameness, weakness, pale gums, increased thirst, increased

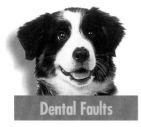

urination, loss of pigmentation on the nose, and ulceration and thickening of the footpads. SLE can affect multiple parts of a dog's system, which makes a definitive diagnosis challenging. Prognosis for dogs with SLE is guarded, at best. Many dogs are euthanized because of the progression and/or severity of the disease, an inability to control it, unacceptable drug reactions, pain, or a severely diminished quality of life.

- **Cutaneous (discoid) Lupus Erythematosus (CLE).** CLE is thought to be a benign or milder form of SLE. Rather than affecting your Aussie's entire body, as SLE does, discoid lupus primarily affects his nose and face. Symptoms include red sores and loss of pigmentation on the nose area. The muzzle area often becomes crusty or scaly. A definitive diagnosis is confirmed through examination of biopsy samples. Prognosis is good, with most dogs living otherwise healthy lives.

Treatment for SLE and CLE varies, but usually consists of corticosteroids or immunosuppressive drugs. The goal is to find a delicate balance—suppress the immune system without opening the door to infection. The mode of inheritance for SLE and CLE is not yet known. Strong evidence suggests genetic factors, and they tend to run in families—meaning your Aussie's brothers, sisters, aunts, uncles, parents, and grandparents may also be affected.

Epilepsy (Idiopathic)

Epilepsy is a term used to describe a disorder of recurring seizures, characterized as either *primary* or *secondary* epilepsy. Secondary epilepsy, also known as acquired or symptomatic epilepsy, refers to seizures for which a cause can be determined. As the name suggests, it is secondary to some kind of identifiable brain damage, such as a stroke, tumor, trauma, metabolic disease, congenital defect, or infection.

Primary (idiopathic) epilepsy refers to recurrent seizures that are of unknown cause. According to experts, "The only thing predictable about idiopathic epilepsy is its unpredictability." Idiopathic epilepsy is considered one of the most common neurologic diseases in dogs, and it is a genetic disease known to affect Australian Shepherds. A strong indication suggests genetic inheritance, although the exact mode of inheritance is not yet known.

No tests confirm epilepsy. Diagnosis is made by ruling out every other possibility. Dogs with epilepsy often have normal laboratory findings, so veterinarians will perform a physical examination and carefully review the dog's medical history and, if available, his seizure history. Dogs with idiopathic epilepsy usually have their first seizure between 1 and 5 years of age.

Canine idiopathic epilepsy is a chronic disease, with no cure. Treatment usually involves anti-epileptic drugs, such as phenobarbital, diazepam, and potassium bromide, to decrease the frequency, severity, and duration of the seizures.

Eye Diseases

Inherited eye diseases are a serious health concern because they can affect your Aussie's vision. They are one of the more common genetic diseases breeders are likely to encounter. Dogs bred from strong conformation lines tend be more heavily affected, but dogs from working lines may experience eye problems, as well. Those most commonly encountered in the Australian Shepherd include:

Cataracts

Like people, dogs get cataracts. They affect nearly every breed, and they are one of the more common eye problems in Australian Shepherds. Yet, there is much scientists still do not know about them. Some cataracts are inherited; others are not. Some are congenital, meaning they are present at birth. (Congenital is frequently confused

Inherited eye diseases are a serious health concern because they can affect your Aussie's vision.

with inherited, but the two terms are completely different.) Some are trauma- or disease-related. Others are developmental, meaning they develop early on in life. Cataracts can also assume a variety of appearances depending on the severity of the situation. They can appear as small white flecks in the eye, which may not cause any visual impairment. In more severe cases, where the opacity is nearly compete and the eye takes on a milky white haze or cloudy appearance, vision loss may range from partial to complete blindness.

Cataracts are classified by several

Cataract Fact

Cataracts differ from nuclear sclerosis, which is a normal change that occurs in the lens of older dogs. Owners frequently mistake the slight graying of the lens as cataracts. Nuclear sclerosis usually occurs in both eyes at the same time and mostly in dogs over the age of 6 years.

factors, including the age of onset and the cause. Affected Aussies usually begin showing signs around 2 or 3 years of age. They are also classified by their location, and the degree of opacity. Most cataracts seen in Aussies are posterior polar, meaning they start in the middle of the backside of the lens.

Your regular veterinarian may be able to confirm the presence of mature or complete cataracts, but a veterinary ophthalmologist is better able to detect small cataracts. No medication is available to prevent, reverse, or shrink cataracts. Surgery is the only known treatment, and new improved microsurgical techniques have increased the success rates of restoring vision to affected Aussies.

Iris Coloboma

A *coloboma* is a fancy word for a gap in part of the structure of the eye. An *iris coloboma* is a gap or missing part of the iris, which is the colored part of your Aussie's eye. The iris either dilates or constricts the pupil to regulate the amount of light entering the eye. In bright light, the pupil is small, but in dim light the pupil is very large to let in as much light as possible. The effect on a dog's vision is minimal. However, a large coloboma can cause your Aussie to squint in bright light because the iris does not contract enough to reduce the amount of light entering the eye.

While the majority of iris colobomas are seen in merle dogs, they are being seen with increasing frequency in non-merle Aussies. While some large colobomas are visible to the naked eye, a canine ophthalmologist can make a definitive diagnosis.

Merle Ocular Dysgenesis

Merle ocular dysgenesis is a group of eye defects found in homozygous merles—dogs who carry two merle genes as a result of breeding a male merle to a female merle. Mathematically, the odds are that one out of every four puppies produced from a merle-to-merle breeding will have either an eye or hearing problem. These defects occur in varying degrees and combinations and include microphthalmia (abnormally small eyes); retinal dysplasia (an abnormal development of the retina, resulting it its folding and detachment); abnormal shape and position of the pupils; irregularities of the iris; cataracts; incomplete development of the optic nerve and blood vessels supplying the eye; and lack of a tapetum (the part of the eye that helps dogs to see at night or in dim lighting).

Breeding merle dogs to merle dogs produces these conditions, so eliminating them is as easy as avoiding merle-to-merle breedings.

Progressive Retinal Atrophy

Progressive retinal atrophy (PRA) has been reported in Aussies, but is considered rare. PRA is the name for several progressive, inherited diseases that lead to blindness. A dog's retina contains photoreceptors called *cones* and *rods*. Rods help a dog see at night or in darkness, while the cones allow a dog to see certain colors. Normally, the photoreceptors in the retina develop after birth to about 8 weeks of age. The retinas of dogs with PRA either have arrested development (retinal dysplasia) or early degeneration of the photoreceptors. PRA worsens over time, with affected dogs generally experiencing night blindness first. Eventually, the condition progresses to failed daytime vision. No treatment is available for PRA.

Hip Dysplasia

Hip dysplasia (HD) is one of the more frequently seen health problems in medium- and large-size breeds and, while not an enormous problem in Aussies, it is worth mentioning. HD is a defect in the conformation of the hip joint that can cause weakness and lameness to a dog's rear quarters, resulting in arthritis, severe

Some Aussies are so driven they will work despite feeling pain.

The British Veterinary Association/Kennel Club (BVA/KC) also x-rays dogs 1 year of age or older. Rather than give a consensus, the BVA/KC separately scores the nine anatomical aspects for each hip. The scores are then added up, totaled, and the dog is given a final rating that ranges from zero, indicating no problems, to 106, which indicates big problems.

debilitating pain, and crippling. Specifically, it is a failure of the head of the femur (thigh bone) to properly fit into the acetabulum (hip bone). The resulting arthritis is frequently referred to as *degenerative joint disease, arthrosis*, or *osteoarthritis*. While it sounds simple, HD is quite complicated, and there is much experts do not yet understand. HD is considered a polygenic inherited disorder, meaning it is controlled by more than one gene. Environmental factors, nutrition, and exercise may also be contributing factors, although this is highly debatable among experts.

Symptoms vary, making it difficult, if not impossible, to predict when or even if a dysplastic Aussie will show symptoms. Some Aussies are very stoic and will continue working regardless of the pain. Others may exhibit mild to severe lameness. Caloric intake, exercise, and weather can influence the appearance of symptoms that may include a decrease in activity, walking or running with an altered gait, resisting movements requiring full extension or flexion of the rear legs, stiffness and pain in the rear legs after exercise or first thing in the morning upon rising, difficulty rising from a lying or sitting position, and balking at stairs. Some dogs may have a swaying, unsteady gait or a "bunny hop" gait in which they run with both hind legs moving together.

A preliminary diagnosis can be made through a combination of a physical examination and x-rays and by ruling out other problems, such as hip and spine disorders, ruptured cruciate ligament, Lyme disease, and so forth. For a definitive evaluation, x-rays can be submitted to the Orthopedic Foundation for Animals (OFA), which grades and certifies the x-rays of dogs over the age of 2 years. The OFA categorizes and grades hips as normal, borderline, or dysplastic.

OFA certification was at one time the most common method of grading a dog's hips. However, the University of Pennsylvania Hip Improvement Program (PennHip) now offers an alternative process using distraction/compression x-rays to obtain accurate and precise measurements of joint laxity, the primary cause of degenerative joint disease. The amount of joint looseness when the dog's hips are completely relaxed is given a distraction index (DI), which strongly correlates to the future development of degenerative joint disease.

Treatment varies and can include nutraceuticals, such as glucosamine, chondroitin, and methylsulfonylmethane (MSM), or over-the-counter drugs, such as buffered aspirin. Your veterinarian may also prescribe a pain reliever. Depending on the age of your

Aussie and the severity of the condition, your veterinarian may recommend surgery, which can include a femoral head ostectomy, triple pelvic osteotomy, or, in some cases, a total hip replacement.

OTHER CANINE HEALTH PROBLEMS

Other health problems that you may encounter with less frequency, but that remain of great concern, include collie eye anomaly, retained testicles, *distichiasis*, elbow dysplasia, and ruptured cruciate ligament.

Collie Eye Anomaly

Originally discovered in Collies (hence its name), Collie eye anomaly (CEA) was once quite common in Aussies, however, breeders have seen a reduced occurrence over the years. CEA is a defect in the formation of the blood vessels and adjacent tissues underlying the retina, causing various eye abnormalities. Experts believe CEA is caused by a single recessive gene, meaning a puppy who inherits one copy of the CEA gene from his mother and one copy from his father will have symptoms of the disease from birth. If he inherits a copy of the CEA gene from only one parent, he will be a *carrier* of the disease but will not show symptoms.

In most cases, dog have pits or notch-like defects in one or both eyes that affect the retina and adjacent tissues. A dog's vision is always impaired, but the extent of impairment depends on the severity of the problem. Some dogs may have limited visual impairment and continue to function quite well. Others will be blind. In severe cases, dogs may have a detached retina, optic nerve abnormalities, and loss of retinal cells. Onset of CEA occurs between 3 and 8 weeks of age and is diagnosed on examination by a canine ophthalmologist.

No treatment for CEA exists. The lesions arise during development, and it is impossible to fix them using current technology. Fortunately, most dogs with CEA have functional vision and live relatively

Breeders have been able to reduce CEA in Aussies.

Cryptorchidism

Cryptorchidism is a hereditary fault affecting male dogs in which one or both testicles do not descend properly into the scrotum. Dogs with one undescended testicle are referred to as being unilateral cryptorchids. These dogs can be fertile and reproduce. Dogs with two undescended testicles are bilateral cryptorchids. These dogs are sterile. Unilateral and bilateral cryptorchids should be neutered.

productive, happy lives. Only a few dogs have complete blindness.

Distichiasis

Distichiasis is a condition in which in small eyelashes abnormally grow on the inner surface or edge of the eyelid. The eyelashes grow inward toward the eye. Left untreated, the abnormal eyelashes can result in scratching and scarring of the cornea. Infections are also common. Treatment usually consists of removal of the eyelashes through surgery or electroepilation.

Elbow Disease

Anatomically, your Aussie's elbow joint is similar to your own elbow. It is a complicated yet efficient hinge-type joint created by the junction of three different bones: the radius, ulna, and humerus. These bones fit and function together with little room for error, and all the parts must work harmoniously for maximum soundness and efficiency. Anything that alters the elbow configuration will affect a dog's ability to use his leg correctly.

Elbow disease—frequently referred to as *elbow dysplasia* or *elbow incongruency*—is really a syndrome for different elbow abnormalities that include ununited anconeal process (UAP), fragmented medial coronoid process (FCP), and osteochondritis desiccans (OCD).

Symptoms of all three diseases are similar and can include a weight-bearing lameness in the front legs that persists for more than a few days, reduction in range of movement, and pain when a veterinarian manipulates the joint. Your veterinarian may recommend a set of x-rays and, in some cases, a computed tomography (CT) scan or exploratory surgery to establish a definitive diagnosis.

Treatment varies, depending on the diagnosis. With FCP and OCD, many experts first recommend medical treatment, which includes a specifically designed exercise program; weight loss, if necessary; and the use of nutraceuticals, such as glucosamine and chondroitin, as well as nonsteroidal anti-inflammatory medications. In some instances of FCP and OCD, surgery may be necessary. UAP is generally treated with surgery.

Cranial Cruciate Ligament (CrCL) Ruptures

Dogs are susceptible to knee injuries, too. A torn knee ligament, specifically the cranial (anterior) cruciate ligament, is one of the more common orthopedic injuries in dogs and the major cause of arthritis of the knee joint. While not an enormous problem in Aussies, it is worth mentioning because direct trauma is a primary cause of CrCL problems in canine athletes. And, if you own an Aussie, you know they are high-energy dogs who move faster than the speed of gossip, which can increase their chance of injury.

A dog's knee (stifle) joint is a fairly complicated joint, but in the simplest of terms it consists of the *femur*, the *tibia*, and the *patella*. The knee joint, unlike the hip and elbow joints, has no interlocking bones. Instead, it relies on an assortment of soft tissue structures to hold everything in place, allowing the knee to bend the way it should, yet keeping it from bending in ways it should not.

The *cranial cruciate ligament* and the *caudal* (posterior) *cruciate ligament* crisscross, forming an X in the knee joint, keeping the femur and tibia from moving back and forth across each other. The CrCL, which provides the most stability to the knee during weight bearing, tends to rupture, allowing the tibia to move excessively in the forward direction, causing joint instability and inflammation of the joint capsule and soft tissues surrounding the joint.

Some breeds appear to be predisposed to CrCL injuries because

Tips for Coping with Hip or Elbow Dysplasia

Hip and elbow dysplasia are primarily inherited conditions, and no products on the market can prevent their development. However, several options may decrease the progression of degenerative joint disease while providing additional comfort to your pet.

- Weight management is essential for your Aussie's overall health. Extra pounds put additional stress on your Aussie's already compromised joints, and overweight Aussies are more susceptible to injuries.
- Exercise your Aussie regularly, but not to excess. Choose exercises that provide good range of motion while limiting wear and tear on the joints, such as walking on surfaces with good traction or swimming. Retrieve or jumping games are hard on a dog's joints and can exacerbate joint problems.
- Orthopedic beds are ideal and provide the necessary cushioning for dogs with sore joints. Equally important, dogs with aches and pains will be able to get on and off an orthopedic bed much more easily than other types of soft, fluffy beds. Be sure the bed is placed in a warm spot away from drafts.
- Like people, dogs love a good massage! Find a good canine chiropractor and make her your best friend. Have her show you a few techniques that you can do at home to help relax your dog's muscles and promote a good range of motion in his joints.
- For dogs with moderate amounts of pain or lameness, consider building or purchasing a ramp so that your Aussie does not need to maneuver steps or stairs. In some cases, stairs or steps may be enough to prevent your dog from getting outside to do his business.

This Aussie's twisting motion can cause CrCL injuries.

of knee conformation or gradual ligament degeneration. However, a torn CrCL in Aussies is frequently a result of direct trauma that occurs at a point when the stifle is turning while in full extension, such as a dog running full speed ahead and suddenly turning, or when a dog slips on a slippery surface or steps in a hole while running.

As with other orthopedic problems, diagnosis involves a physical examination, manipulation of the joint, and observation of joint movement. X-rays can help provide a definitive diagnosis, and surgery is generally the most common method of correction. The longer the knee goes untreated, the greater the chance of irreversible arthritic conditions developing.

EXTERNAL PARASITES

Parasites. They sound grotesque and, to the average dog owner, they usually are. Unfortunately, it is highly likely that sometime within your Australian Shepherd's life he will suffer from parasites, and you will need to deal with them. If left unchecked, parasites can cause debilitating and life-threatening problems.

Demodectic Mange

Demodectic mange is a skin disease caused by a microscopic mite, *Demodex canis*. In small numbers, these mites are typically present on your dog's skin and, in most cases, usually cause no problems.

Demodicosis' development is complex and not completely understood, but here's what experts do know: Small numbers of Demodex mites normally inhabit the hair follicles and sebaceous glands of dogs; these are passed from a mother to a puppy, usually through contact when nursing, during the first week of life. Veterinarians believe the tendency to develop demodicosis may be an inherited problem—some dogs are born with an ineffective or sensitive immune system that in turn interferes with the dog's ability to keep the mites under control. As a result, the dog develops mange. Systemic disease, estrus, and heartworm infection can also predispose a dog to generalized demodicosis.

Two forms of the disease exist: localized and generalized. Localized demodicosis is the most common, occurring in dogs under 1 year of age and involving five or fewer lesions. Lesions can appear as crusty, red skin with hair loss, and may have a greasy or moist appearance. Most lesions are confined to the muzzle, eyes, and other areas around the head, and usually clear up as the puppy grows and develops his own immunity. Your vet may suggest shampoos, dips, and topical ointments or creams. Prognosis is good, with 90 percent of dogs recovering without treatment. Ten percent develop the more severe, generalized form.

Dogs with generalized demodicosis typically experience lesions and hair loss over the entire body, red skin, and lesions on the head, neck, stomach, legs, and feet. A secondary bacterial infection, the disease's worst part, aggravates the lesions. In severe cases, dogs become quiet ill, developing lethargy, fever, and loss of appetite. A definitive diagnosis is made by clinical diagnosis of lesions and skin scrapings to confirm the presence of mites. All dogs have mites, so the visual identification of lesions is important. Veterinarians also look for causes of a suppressed immune system, such as hypothyroidism, Cushing's disease, diabetes, or cancer.

Generalized cases require a more aggressive approach including insecticidal dips, anti-parasitic drugs, antibiotics, and follow-up vet visits every 4 to 6 weeks to assess infection and sometimes revise therapy.

The prognosis depends on the dog's age at the time he develops the disease. After treatment, puppies have less than a 50 percent chance of recurrence. Adult dogs usually require lifetime treatment, with success dependent on the dog's medication tolerance, any

Most owners will have to deal with fleas at some point.

underlying causes, and the owner's commitment to treatment.

Fleas

If you own an Australian Shepherd, you no doubt know a thing or two about fleas. One bite from these pesky creatures can cause itching for days. And where one flea exists, it's a safe bet there are plenty more looming in your carpet, furniture, bedding, and on your precious Australian Shepherd! What you may not know is over 2,200 species of fleas exist worldwide.

In North America, *Ctenocephalides felis*, the domestic cat flea, likes both cats and dogs. It is the most common flea responsible for wreaking havoc with your precious pooch. About 1/8-inch long, slightly smaller than a sesame seed, and generally brown or black in color, these wingless bloodsuckers are responsible for spreading tapeworms to dogs and causing serious allergy dermatitis. In serious infestations, fleas can cause anemia, especially in puppies.

Flea Allergy Dermatitis

If your Australian Shepherd is sensitive to fleas, one bite from this tiny, nearly invisible pest can make his life (and yours!) miserable, plunging him into a vicious cycle of biting, scratching, and licking. Flea allergy dermatitis, also known as bite hypersensitivity, tends to be most prevalent during the summer when fleas are most rampant and annoying.

Getting Rid of Fleas

The advent of once-a-month topical treatments makes eradicating fleas a breeze compared to 15 years ago. You mustn't become complacent, however. You must keep on top of the pesky buggers. If you live where the temperatures dip to freezing, count your blessings. The cat flea is susceptible to cold—it can't survive when exposed to temperatures below roughly 37° F (3° C).

To control and eliminate fleas, try these steps:

Clean everything your dog has come in contact with. Wash his dog beds and blankets and mop up floors. Vacuum all carpets, rugs, and furniture. Immediately dispose of vacuum bags, because eggs can hatch in them.

If necessary, remove dense vegetation near your home, dog yard, or kennel area—these spaces offer a damp microenvironment favorable to flea development.

Treat your Aussie and any other household pets that can serve as hosts, such as other dogs, cats, and ferrets.

A number of proven effective insecticides and insect growth regulators are available for use in the home. Some of these insecticides are toxic. Read all labels and follow directions carefully.

A number of on-animal flea control products are available, such as shampoos, sprays, dips, powders, and flea collars. Many of these products have been around for years, but remember that many commercial and natural products may be toxic. They may irritate your Aussie's skin or cause health problems.

Fleas feeding on your Aussie inject saliva that contains different antigens and histamine-like substances, resulting in irritation and itching sensations that can range from mild to downright nasty. Dogs with flea allergies usually itch over their entire bodies, experience generalized hair loss, and develop red, inflamed skin and hot spots. Frequently restless and uncomfortable, they usually spend the majority of their time scratching, digging, licking, and chewing their skin. It's a miserable and agonizing situation.

Check your dog for ticks after he's been outside.

Treatments vary and can be multifaceted. Of primary importance is a strict flea control program to prevent additional infestation. Veterinarians frequently recommend hypoallergenic or colloidal oatmeal-type shampoos to remove allergens, and topical anti-itch creams to soothe the skin. These products can provide immediate, short-term relief, but they are not always a long-term solution. Fatty acid supplements, such as omega-3 and -6 found in flaxseed and fish oils, are proving helpful in reducing the amount and effects of histamine. In some cases, veterinarians prescribe corticosteroids to reduce itching.

Ticks

Approximately 850 species of these blood-sucking parasites exist. Ticks burrow into your Aussie's skin and engorge themselves with blood, expanding to many times their original size. They are dangerous because they can secrete a paralysis-causing toxin and can spread serious diseases such as Lyme disease, Rocky Mountain spotted fever, Texas fever, tularemia, babesiosis, and canine ehrlichiosis. Ticks can be infected with and transmit more than one disease, so it's not uncommon to see a dog infected with more than one disease at a time. In severe infestations, anemia and even death may occur.

Your Aussie is most likely to pick up ticks in wooded or grassy areas and overgrown fields. Ticks commonly embed themselves between the toes, in the ears, and around the neck, but they can be found elsewhere on the body. Each species has its own favored feeding sites on your Aussie.

Controlling ticks on your Aussie is similar to the process for controlling fleas. Some of the once-a-month topical treatments for

Removing an attached tick is not terribly difficult—once you get past any queasiness about doing so.

Always use a pair of tweezers or a specially designed tick-removing tool. Small curved hemostats or curved-tip jeweler tweezers also work well.

Grasp the tick as close as possible to where it enters your dog's skin.

Pull slowly, firmly, and steadily in an outward direction. Don't jerk, squeeze, or twist the tick.

After removing the tick, place it in a jar of alcohol to kill it. Some experts recommend keeping the tick alive in a sealed, dated vial for at least 1 month in case symptoms of tick-borne diseases develop. You can discuss this option with your veterinarian.

A small welt or skin reaction may occur once a tick is removed. Clean the bite wound with a disinfectant. If you want, apply an antibiotic ointment.

If you simply cannot bring yourself to remove a tick, take the dog to your veterinarian. Ticks must be removed, and the sooner the better.

fleas also kill ticks, but check with your veterinarian first. Just as with eradicating fleas, you must treat your yard, house, doghouse, dog blankets, and your dog with a product specifically designed for ticks. Over-the-counter products such as sprays, foggers, powders, dips, shampoos, and collars are available. Ticks are not as susceptible to cold weather as fleas, so you must treat your yard late into the fall and early winter. Again, many of these products may be toxic, so read all labels and follow directions carefully. When in doubt, consult your veterinarian before purchasing and using any tick-control products.

Avoid tick-infested areas during the peak tick season. When walking your Aussie, do not allow him to wander off designated paths or near low-hanging branches and shrubs where ticks are likely to be waiting for an unsuspecting Aussie to pass by.

INTERNAL PARASITES

Internal parasites are called *endoparasites* because they live inside your Australian Shepherd's body. Heartworms, hookworms, roundworms, tapeworms, and whipworms are the most common. Deworming medications are available at local pet stores and retail outlets; however, they differ drastically in their safety and effectiveness in expelling worms from the body. The wisest choice is to have a veterinarian diagnose the specific type of internal parasite and prescribe the proper deworming medication.

Heartworms

Heartworms, found throughout the United States, are potentially the most dangerous internal parasite. Mosquitoes transmit the disease when they suck blood from an infected dog and then bite a healthy dog, thereby depositing larvae. The larvae grow inside the healthy dog, migrating through the tissues into the bloodstream and eventually into the heart. The larvae grow into adult worms between 6 and 14 inches (15 and 36 cm) long. The process is relatively slow and can take about 6 to 7 months from the time the dog is bitten until an adult heartworm develops. A severely infected dog can have several hundred heartworms in his heart and vessels, completely filling and obstructing the heart chambers and the various large blood vessels leading from the heart to the lungs.

Dogs with heartworm infections may not show symptoms until the damage is extensive and the disease is well advanced. First symptoms usually include a chronic cough, followed by a decrease in appetite, loss of weight, listlessness, and fatigue after light exercise. Some dogs accumulate fluid in their abdomens and take on a pot-bellied appearance. In rare situations, the dog may die of sudden heart failure.

Diagnosis is usually made using a blood test that detects the presence of antigens in the blood. Preventive medications are available and highly recommended, but they must never be given to a dog who is already infected with worms. It is imperative that you consult with your veterinarian before starting any preventive treatment for heartworms.

Treatment can be successful if the infestation is diagnosed early. However, it is not without risk because some—but not all—of the drugs used to kill the adult worms contain arsenic. The death of the worms can also create blood clots, which present their own life-threatening problems. The protocol your veterinarian chooses will depend on the severity of infection, and whether or not your Australian Shepherd's kidney and liver functions can tolerate the treatment.

Your vet will determine the best course to treat internal parasites.

Hookworms

Hookworms are only about 1/2-inch (1.3 cm) long, but they can cause serious health problems for your Aussie including diarrhea, vomiting, and life-threatening anemia. Your Aussie's gums may appear pale, he may be weak, and his stools may appear black and tarry. In severe cases, a blood transfusion may be necessary.

Adult hookworms have teeth-like structures (hooks) that attach to the lining of your Aussie's intestine, feeding on his oxygen-carrying blood. They damage the lining, then migrate to a new location, leaving the old wound to continue bleeding. They lay eggs that are passed in the dog's feces, where they hatch into larvae. Infection occurs when larvae enter through your dog's skin and migrate to the intestinal tract. An Aussie can also become infected if he ingests contaminated food or water or licks his contaminated feet. A puppy can become infected when larvae migrate to the uterus or mammary glands of a pregnant bitch, thereby infecting the

Australian Shepherds can have life-threatening reactions to drugs such as ivermectin (found in heartworm preventatives) and Imodium (an over-the-counter antidiarrheal). Experts at Washington State University's College of Veterinary Medicine believe the culprit is a mutant gene that does not pump the drug out of the dog's brain, causing abnormal neurological signs, serious illness, and even death. Testing is available through the University, and is highly recommended.

fetuses or nursing puppies.

People can pick up hookworms, too, which makes sanitary practices doubly important. All fecal material should be removed daily. When walking in public places, do not allow your dog to come in contact with other dogs' feces.

Roundworms

A common parasite of the canine digestive tract, roundworms (often called ascarids) live in a dog's small intestine. Occasionally found in adult dogs and people, they are most common in puppies, with most puppies requiring deworming at an early age. Puppies usually become infected when the larvae pass through the mother's uterus or milk, although Aussies also can become infected when they eat an infected animal, such as a rodent, ingest soil contaminated with roundworms, come in contact with infected feces, or snack from the cat's litter box.

Roundworms absorb nutrients, interfere with digestion, and can damage the lining of a dog's intestine. In more severe infestations, your puppy may be thin and have a potbellied appearance. His coat may be dry, dull, and rough looking. Some puppies have intestinal discomfort and cry as a result. Diarrhea or constipation and vomiting are also frequent symptoms. In some cases, a cough may develop due to the migration of the larvae through the respiratory system.

Roundworm eggs are resistant to environmental conditions and most common disinfectants. They can adhere to hair, skin, and paws, so good hygiene and strict sanitation are important to minimize further contamination. Feces should be picked up daily. Once roundworms get into your soil, they can live for months or years. Tilling the soil to a depth of 8 to 12 inches, removing it and replacing it with new soil, or paving the entire area is about the only way to totally solve the problem.

Tapeworms

While generally not life-threatening, tapeworms are a problem because they attach to your dog's intestinal wall to absorb nutrients. They are segmented and consist of a head, neck, and a number of segments that contain large numbers of eggs that break away from the rest of the worm and are passed in the feces. These are sometimes visible on the dog's anus or in his stools. Some dogs will scoot their rear ends along the ground.

Unlike the whipworms, roundworms, and hookworms, tapeworms must go through an intermediate host, with fleas and lice being the most common intermediate host in dogs and cats. Tapeworms are acquired when a dog ingests an intermediate host. In certain species of tapeworms, rabbits and livestock can be the intermediate hosts. While less common, infections can occur when dogs eat or scavenge the internal body parts of wild game or the discarded parts of butchered livestock, or are given raw meat.

Tapeworms generally do not cause any symptoms, although diarrhea may be present. In severe infestations, your Aussie may exhibit abdominal discomfort or nervousness. Getting rid of tapeworms requires successfully eliminating the head of the tapeworm, otherwise it will regrow a new body. Flea and lice control are essential, otherwise your Australian Shepherd will continue to reinfest himself.

Whipworms

Whipworms get their name from the whiplike shape of the adult worm. Dogs become infected when they ingest food, grass, or water that is contaminated with whipworm eggs. If your Aussie buries his bone in the dirt, he can pick up eggs from the infected soil. The eggs are swallowed, hatch in his large intestine and, in about 3 months, the larvae mature into adults that attach to the intestinal lining and burrow their mouths into the intestinal wall where they feed on blood. Adult worms lay eggs that are passed in the feces.

Keep your backyard clean so playtime can be safe and fun.

The symptoms vary depending on the number of worms in a dog's intestines. Mild infestations may produce no obvious symptoms in healthy individuals. Larger infestations, however, can result in diarrhea, mucus and blood in the stools, loss of weight, and inflammation of the intestinal wall. Anemia is possible if hemorrhaging into the intestine occurs.

Detecting whipworms can be difficult because whipworms

do not continually shed eggs. A negative stool sample does not mean your Aussie does not have whipworms. It simply means no eggs were found in that sample. Stool samples collected on multiple days may be necessary for positive identification.

Whipworms can live in moist soil for years, and they are resistant to freezing. However, dry conditions, good drainage, sunlight, and aeration of kennels, dog runs, and exercise areas destroy whipworm eggs. Like roundworms, soil contamination is a serious problem. To help reduce or prevent contamination, pick up fecal matter daily and thoroughly clean kennels or dog run areas. If possible, allow these areas to dry in direct sunlight.

PROTOZOAL INTESTINAL INFECTIONS

Protozoa are one-celled organisms or parasites that infect the intestinal tract of dogs. Two of the most common protozoal infections that affect Australian Shepherds are coccidiosis and giardiasis.

Coccidia

Spread in the feces of carrier animals, *Coccidia* are a group of protozoan parasites that invade the cells of your Aussie's small intestine. They multiply rapidly, destroying tissue. Once infected, the disease is referred to as coccidiosis. *Coccidia* are most common in puppies younger than 6 months of age, adult dogs with suppressed immune systems, and dogs who are under physiological stress, such as change of ownership, shipping, weaning, overcrowding, fatigue, dietary changes, or when other diseases are present. Young Aussie's may experience diarrhea streaked with blood, weight loss, diminished appetite, and, in some instances, even death.

By far the most common method of infection in young puppies is exposure to their mother's infected feces or to the environment. Cockroaches and flies can carry *Coccidia* from one location to another, and an Aussie who eats mice or other animals infected with *Coccidia* can become infected.

Coccidiosis is highly contagious, and any infected puppy is contagious to other puppies. Controlling the spread of coccidiosis requires strict sanitary practices. Fecal matter should be removed daily. Water and food should be housed so it cannot become contaminated with feces. This helps reduce the potential for infection, but does not guarantee that infections will not occur. The good news is that coccidiosis is treatable with prescription drugs.

Giardia

Giardia live in the small intestine of dogs. Infection with *Giardia* is called giardiasis. The microscopic parasites reproduce by dividing in half many times. After an unknown number of divisions, they are passed in the stool. Giardiasis has been nicknamed the "backpackers' disease" because it is commonly acquired by drinking infected water in high mountain lakes and streams. Beavers are most often blamed for contaminating the water by passing the intestinal organism in their feces. *Giardia* can also be tracked into your house or kennel on your shoes or boots.

Giardia prevent proper absorption of nutrients, damage the intestinal lining, and interfere with digestion. In many cases involving adult dogs, few symptoms appear. Younger dogs may develop diarrhea or abnormal, soft, or light-colored stools that have a bad odor and greasy appearance. Some dogs will not lose their appetite, but they may lose weight.

Modern technology makes giardiasis easier to diagnose, which, of course, allows veterinarians to begin treating the problem much earlier. Veterinarians differ in their treatment because currently no drugs are approved for treating giardiasis in dogs. Often, treatment is given to control secondary infection.

Alternative Medicine

Alternative medicine is a broad term used to describe anything other than conventional medical treatments and practices. Traditional medicine is rooted in science, physics, chemistry, and biology, and its practices are backed by scientific data. While some alternative medicine has been around for thousands of years, it is empirical, meaning the evidence comes less from clinical trials and more from the anecdotes and testimonials of veterinarians and dog owners. As the demand for alternative medicine for humans has grown, so too has the demand for alternative veterinary medicine, which is sometimes referred to as *complementary and alternative veterinary medicine* (CAVM).

Alternative medicine encompasses a broad range of treatments including:

- Acupuncture
- Chiropractic
- Massage
- Herb, natural supplements, and vitamin and mineral supplementation
- Homeopathy

The American Veterinary Medical Association has established guidelines for veterinary acupuncture, chiropractic, homeopathic, and holistic medicine. *Alternative* and *herbal* do not mean harmless. The U.S. Food and Drug Administration (FDA) does not regulate herbs and natural supplements. They can cause side effects or result in cross-reactions if combined with other supplements or medications. To prevent problems, always consult your veterinarian.

Do your best to stay calm during emergencies.

FIRST AID

Dogs, especially Aussies, have the uncanny ability to get into anything and everything and always at the most inopportune and unexpected times. If your Aussie is sick or injured, always err on the side of caution and contact your veterinarian or 24-emergency clinic pronto. Many minor situations, such as scrapes, nicks, abrasions, or a bout of diarrhea, can be successfully treated at home, coupled with a "wait and see" attitude—provided you are able to recognize the difference between a minor situation and a life-threatening medical emergency.

Life-Threatening Symptoms

If your dog has any of these symptoms, seek medical assistance right away:

- Bleeding that is heavy or can't be stopped
- Breathing that is difficult or labored, or no breathing at all
- Collapse, coma, depression, extreme lethargy, or unconsciousness
- Diarrhea that is uncontrolled or bloody, or stools that are black and tarry
- Gums that are bluish or white
- Lethargy
- No pulse or heart beat
- Pain
- Seizures
- Temperature over 105°F (41° C). The average body temperature for a dog is 101.5° F (38.6° C).
- Vomiting blood or uncontrolled vomiting
- Teeth that are broken, bleeding, or loose

Seek immediate veterinary assistance if your dog has been exposed to trauma, poisoning, or gastrointestinal distress including:

- Bite from a snake, poisonous spider, toad, or another animal—especially a cat or unvaccinated animal
- Electrocution (i.e., chewing on an electrical cord)

- Excessive heat or cold
- Overdose of medications
- Porcupine quills embedded in the skin
- Puncture wounds
- Trauma of any kind—hit by a car; kicked by a horse; falling from an open window, the bed of a pickup, balcony, etc.
- Swallowing a foreign object (toy, marble, paperclip, sock, etc.)

This is a small sampling of the things that can go wrong when you own an Australian Shepherd. Prevention is always the best route. However, in spite of your best intentions, accidents do happen, so familiarize yourself with the various emergency-response protocols. A number of canine first-aid books and videos are available through retail outlets and online. If possible, attend a canine first-aid seminar and have a canine first-aid kit on hand. You can purchase pre-assembled kits or assemble your own. Equally important, you should post in a conspicuous spot the following numbers:

- ASPCA Poison Control Hotline 1-888-426-4435 (a fee is charged to your credit card)

What's In a First Aid Kit?

First aid kits vary in their content. Some contain enough medical paraphernalia to perform minor surgeries. Others are mini kits that clip on your belt for walks in the park, hiking, etc. Home kits contain basic first-aid equipment. Whether you choose to purchase a super colossal pre-assembled kit, a basic home kit, or customize your own, it should contain basic necessities including:

- Activated charcoal (available from pharmacists; it binds or neutralizes certain poisons)
- Alcohol or alcohol prep pads (for sterilizing scissors, tweezers; not for use on wounds)
- Anti-diarrheal medicine (Aussies can have adverse reactions to Imodium.)
- Aspirin (not nonsteroidal anti-inflammatory drugs, such as acetaminophen or ibuprofen)
- Eye wash or saline solution (for flushing out eye contaminants)
- Eye ointment
- Gauze rolls and gauze pads
- Gloves (disposable latex for protecting hands, prevent contamination of wounds)
- Hydrogen peroxide 3% USP
- Instant cold pack and instant heat wrap
- Iodine (for cleaning wounds)
- Ipecac (to induce vomiting, if necessary)
- Lubricant (mineral oil or KY Jelly)
- Muzzle (a dog may try to bite if he is injured or scared)
- Ointments (triple antibiotic ointment inhibits bacterial growth in cuts, abrasions)
- Pill gun (for administering pills)
- Rehydrating solutions (to replace lost electrolytes)
- Scissors (to clip hair around wounds, cut gauze, etc.)
- Styptic pencil (stops bleeding if a nail is broken, torn, clipped too short)
- Thermometer (preferably digital)
- Tick-removal tool
- Turkey baster, bulb syringe, or large medical syringe (for flushing wounds)
- Tweezers
- Wraps (self-clinging, flexible elastic-type bandages for wrapping injuries)

- Your veterinarian's number
- A 24-hour emergency veterinary clinic (in the event your vet's office is closed)
- The local animal control office in case your dog is lost

When calling the Poison Control Hotline, tell the operator the type of poison ingested, the amount, the duration since ingestion, and any symptoms your dog is experiencing. You will also need your Australian Shepherd's age, sex, and weight.

EMERGENCIES

Hopefully, you will never have to deal with anything more serious than bumps and bruises. However, owning an Aussie means you must to be prepared for certain emergencies.

Choking

Dogs can choke on any number of items from disemboweled doll parts, buttons, safety pins, and dog bones. Some Australian Shepherds choke on their food if they wolf it down too quickly. Any obstruction of your dog's airway is a life-threatening medical emergency and must be dealt with immediately to prevent brain damage or death.

The symptoms of choking vary; however, the most common signs include a coughing, gagging, or retching noise, and pawing at the side of the face. His tongue may turn blue, and he may collapse. If your Aussie can get some air around the obstruction, seek veterinary attention immediately.

If he cannot get air around the obstruction, work on clearing his airway. If possible, pull your Aussie's lower jaw open and tilt his head upward. If an object is visible, try to remove it with your finger without pushing it deeper. Use extreme caution to avoid being bitten. Regardless of how friendly your dog might be, a panicked, choking dog is likely to bite as a reflex mechanism.

Keep an eye on your Aussie when he is out in extreme temperatures.

The Heimlich Maneuver for Dogs

If the object cannot be removed easily, a Heimlich-type maneuver can be performed on dogs. Become familiar with the procedure before a medical emergency arises. It may mean the difference between life and death for your Aussie. Your veterinarian can show you how to perform the procedure.

A kiddie pool can keep your Aussie cool on a hot day.

- **For an adult or large dog:** Hold your dog from behind, wrap your arms around his body just behind the ribs. Wrap one hand around the other to make a double fist, placing the double fist on his abdomen below the rib cage. Squeeze sharply a few times, quickly pressing upward and forward until the object is expelled or dislodged.

- **For puppies or small dogs:** Follow the above procedure, but rather than use a double fist, place the index and middle fingers of both hands on the puppy's abdomen below the rib cage. Press into the abdomen with a quick, upward thrust. It may take several tries to dislodge or expel the object.

Once you have cleared your dog's airway, have him examined by a veterinarian as soon as possible.

Diarrhea

Diarrhea can occur if you overfeed your dog, if you change his normal food from one brand to another too quickly, or if there is a change in water while traveling. (That's why it is always prudent to carry your own water or purchase bottled water.) Unclean feeding bowls, stress, and allergies can also cause diarrhea. It can also be a symptom of intestinal parasites or disease.

Equally important, you should know what your Aussie's normal stool look like. When you know what is normal, you are more likely to recognize when something is not right. Normal feces vary in color and consistency depending on the individual dog and his diet. Normal color usually ranges from light brown to dark brown. If the diarrhea is slight, and your dog has no other symptoms, it may be nothing more than minor gastric upset. Withholding food for 24 hours, and then feeding a mixture of cooked white rice and boiled chicken or extra lean hamburger browned in a skillet with any excess grease removed may

Australian Shepherds need not run around like wild banshees in the heat of the day to be susceptible to heatstroke. Non-exertion heatstroke most commonly occurs when dogs are confined in an overheated enclosure, such as an automobile, or when they are confined outdoors during warm weather or high humidity and deprived of water or shade.

correct the problem. Medications such as bismuth subsalicylate (Pepto-Bismol) or kaolin/pectin (Kaopectate) every 4 hours may also fix the problem. Remember, Aussies can have severe reactions to certain over-the-counter anti-diarrhea medications, so always consult a veterinarian before giving him any human medications. A veterinarian will be able to give you the correct dosage, as well. If you have a puppy or older dog with diarrhea, if the diarrhea is black or green, or your dog is showing other signs of illness, call your veterinarian right away.

Heat-Induced Illnesses

The average dog's body temperature is 101.5° F (38.6° C), with a normal range between 100° and 102° (37° C and 39° C). These are core temperatures, based on rectal thermometer readings. While temperatures can vary throughout a dog's body, the core temperature is one of several constant internal (homeostatic) conditions, which also include blood pressure and blood chemistry. Heat-induced illnesses occur when a dog's normal body mechanisms cannot keep his core temperature within a safe range.

Unlike humans, dogs do not sweat. Their primary cooling mechanisms are panting and conduction. When overheated dogs pant, they breathe in and out through their mouths. They inhale cool air and, as the air moves into their lungs, it absorbs heat and moisture. When they exhale, the hot air passes over their wet tongues and evaporation occurs, enhancing and maximizing heat loss and cooling their bodies.

Conduction, the second method of cooling, occurs when a dog lies down on a cool surface, such as a tile floor, grass, or wet concrete. The heat from his body is transferred to the cool surface.

Four types of heat-induced illnesses can occur: heat cramps, heat exhaustion, heat prostration, and heatstroke. Heat cramps are muscle cramps caused by the loss of salt from a dog's system and by extreme exertion in hot weather. They do not normally occur in dogs, and it is unlikely you will encounter them in an Australian Shepherd. The specific heat-related health issues must be aware of are heat exhaustion, heat prostration, and heatstroke.

Heat Exhaustion

Heat exhaustion is the least severe of the heat-related illnesses. However, it must be taken seriously. Often referred to as a mild case of heatstroke, it is characterized by lethargy and an inability to perform normal activities or work, such as obedience, agility, or tracking because of extreme heat.

Heat Prostration

Heat prostration is the next level and is considered a moderate case of heatstroke with a the dog's body temperature at 104° F to 106° F (40° C to 41° C). Possible signs include rapid panting, red or pale gums, weakness, vomiting, mental confusion, and dizziness. Seek immediate veterinary attention. Dogs with a moderate case of heatstroke can often recover without complicating health problems.

Heatstroke

Heatstroke is the most severe form of heat prostration and occurs when a dog's body temperatures is over 106° F (41° C). Dogs suffering from heatstroke display signs that include rapid panting, collapsing, inability to stand up, red or pale gums, thick and sticky saliva, weakness, vomiting (with or without blood), diarrhea, shock, fainting, or coma. This is a life-threatening medical emergency that can result in multiple organ system dysfunction, including the respiratory, cardiovascular, gastrointestinal, renal, and central nervous systems. Immediate veterinary assistance is essential.

What You Can Do

The best defense against heatstroke is to monitor your dog and his activities. Do not place him in a situation where he can become overheated. Limit exercise, such as running, playing, herding, and training to the cooler parts of the day. If your dog is experiencing symptoms of heatstroke, get him to a cool environment immediately. Lower his temperature by submerging his body in cool (not cold) water (keep his head elevated above the water) or applying cool water to his body with a shower or hose. If he will drink on his own, give him water or a rehydrating solution. Do not force water, because he is likely to choke. Place him on a wet towel to keep him cool, and get medical assistance immediately.

Strenuous exercise can lead to heat related illnesses.

On a sunny day when ambient temperatures are 86° F (30° C), the internal temperature of a parked vehicle can quickly reach 134° F to 154° F (56.6° C to 67.7° C) even with all the windows partly open. A dog can suffer irreparable brain damage or death if his body temperature rises to 107° F (41.6° C). In the amount of time it takes to make a quick trip into the grocery store, your Australian Shepherd could be exposed to life-threatening temperatures.

Poisoning

So goes the saying, "an ounce of prevention…." Prevention is always the best route, but let's face it, accidents do happen despite your best intentions. If you suspect your Aussie has come in contact with a poisonous substance, treat it as a medical emergency. Do not delay—seek immediate veterinary attention. If you see your dog eating or drinking a poisonous substance, do not wait for symptoms to develop. Call the Poison Control Center or take your dog to the nearest veterinary clinic. Do not induce vomiting unless instructed by a veterinarian.

Treatment varies depending on the type of poison ingested. Take with you, if possible, the remains of the toxic product, be it a half-eaten plant, a mangled snail bait package, a leaking herbicide bottle, or an empty box of chocolates. If your dog has vomited, scoop up the remains and take it with you. It can provide the veterinarian with important clues regarding the type of poison your dog ingested.

Vomiting

Dogs vomit occasionally and, unlike humans, they so with little discomfort. They vomit when they get excited, drink too much water too fast (especially after exercise), gulp their food, when they go for a ride in the car, or after they've eaten grass. If your dog appears to be healthy, a single vomiting incident should not send you rushing to the vet. It may be nothing more than a simple upset stomach. Keep him away from any food for a few hours. Allow him small amounts of water, but don't let him gulp water. Nothing makes a vomiting dog vomit more than a tummy full of water or food. If the problem persists, especially with puppies or old dogs, or if your dog has other symptoms, such as diarrhea, stomach bloating, listlessness, labored breathing, pain, or you see blood or abnormal material in the vomit, contact your veterinarian right away. And don't forget to take a sample of the vomit with you.

THE SENIOR AUSTRALIAN SHEPHERD

Australian Shepherds are considered "seniors" anywhere from age 9 and older. You are the best judge of when to make this call for your dog. You will notice when he begins to slow down, is not interested in long walks around the neighborhood, sleeps more, and seems to be getting gray around the muzzle. Your veterinarian may also notice signs that indicate it is time to consider these your dog's golden years.

Many owners say that this time of their dogs' life is the most enjoyable because their dogs have a routine, they know the family, and they know what to expect. Older dogs tend to be less active, which means you do not need to keep up with them , and they are more interested than ever in curling up next to you on the couch.

Old age has its requirements, though, just as puppyhood did. You must assess your dog's overall health and determine what's needed to maintain it as its peak. This may mean changing his diet to one specially formulated for seniors. It may mean supplementing his food with certain vitamins, minerals, or herbs for improved skin condition or healthier joints. It may mean your dog needs to wear a sweater in cool weather and a coat when it's cold.

Mind how you interact with your senior citizen. His eyesight or hearing may be failing before it is readily apparent; be sure he hears and sees you when asking him to do things so you don't get upset with him. His bladder control may weaken, leading to accidents in the house. These are probably as upsetting to him as to you; have patience—remember, your friend won't live forever. Treasure him while you can!

Keeping your Aussie in good health will help create a partnership for many years.

ASSOCIATIONS AND ORGANIZATIONS

Breed Clubs

American Herding Breed Association
www.ahba-herding.org

American Kennel Club (AKC)
5580 Centerview Drive
Raleigh, NC 27606
Telephone: (919) 233-9767
Fax: (919) 233-3627
E-mail: info@akc.org
www.akc.org

Australian Shepherd Club of America (ASCA)
6091 E. State Hwy 21
Bryan, TX 778-9-9652
Telephone: (979) 778-1082
E-mail: manager@asca.org
www.asca.org

Canadian Kennel Club (CKC)
89 Skyway Avenue, Suite 100
Etobicoke, Ontario M9W 6R4
Telephone: (416) 675-5511
Fax: (416) 675-6506
E-mail: information@ckc.ca
www.ckc.ca

Federation Cynologique Internationale (FCI)
Secretariat General de la FCI
Place Albert 1er, 13
B – 6530 Thuin
Belqique
www.fci.be

International Sheep Dog Society (ISDS)
Clifton House
4a Goldington Road
Bedford
MK40 3NF
Telephone: 44 (0) 1234 352672
Fax: 44 (0) 1234 348214
E-mail: office@isds.org.uk
www.isds.org.uk

The Kennel Club
1 Clarges Street
London
W1J 8AB
Telephone: 0870 606 6750
Fax: 0207 518 1058
www.the-kennel-club.org.uk

United Kennel Club (UKC)
100 E. Kilgore Road
Kalamazoo, MI 49002-5584
Telephone: (269) 343-9020
Fax: (269) 343-7037
E-mail: pbickell@ukcdogs.com
www.ukcdogs.com

United States Australian Shepherd Association (USASA)
Membership Information:
Rhonda J. Diercks
Email: PAaussie@comcast.net
www.australianshepherds.org

Pet Sitters

National Association of Professional Pet Sitters
15000 Commerce Parkway, Suite C
Mt. Laurel, New Jersey 08054
Telephone: (856) 439-0324
Fax: (856) 439-0525
E-mail: napps@ahint.com
www.petsitters.org

Pet Sitters International
201 East King Street
King, NC 27021-9161
Telephone: (336) 983-9222
Fax: (336) 983-5266
E-mail: info@petsit.com
www.petsit.com

Rescue Organizations and Animal Welfare Groups

American Humane Association (AHA)
63 Inverness Drive East
Englewood, CO 80112
Telephone: (303) 792-9900
Fax: 792-5333
www.americanhumane.org

American Society for the Prevention of Cruelty to Animals (ASPCA)
424 E. 92nd Street
New York, NY 10128-6804
Telephone: (212) 876-7700
www.aspca.org

Royal Society for the Prevention of Cruelty to Animals (RSPCA)
Telephone: 0870 3335 999
Fax: 0870 7530 284
www.rspca.org.uk

The Humane Society of the United States (HSUS)
2100 L Street, NW
Washington DC 20037
Telephone: (202) 452-1100
www.hsus.org

Sports

Canine Freestyle Federation, Inc.
Secretary: Brandy Clymire
E-Mail: secretary@canine-freestyle.org
www.canine-freestyle.org

International Agility Link (IAL)
Global Administrator: Steve Drinkwater
E-mail: yunde@powerup.au
www.agilityclick.com/~ial

North American Dog Agility Council
11522 South Hwy 3
Cataldo, ID 83810
www.nadac.com

North American Flyball Association
www.flyball.org
1400 West Devon Avenue #512
Chicago, IL 6066
800-318-6312

United States Dog Agility Association
P.O. Box 850955
Richardson, TX 75085-0955
Telephone: (972) 487-2200
www.usdaa.com

World Canine Freestyle Organization
P.O. Box 350122
Brooklyn, NY 11235-2525
Telephone: (718) 332-8336
www.worldcaninefreestyle.org

Therapy

Delta Society
875 124th Ave NE, Suite 101
Bellevue, WA 98005
Telephone: (425) 226-7357
Fax: (425) 235-1076
E-mail: info@deltasociety.org
www.deltasociety.org

Therapy Dogs Incorporated
PO Box 5868
Cheyenne, WY 82003
Telephone: (877) 843-7364
E-mail: therdog@sisna.com
www.therapydogs.com

Therapy Dogs International (TDI)
88 Bartley Road
Flanders, NJ 07836
Telephone: (973) 252-9800
Fax: (973) 252-7171
E-mail: tdi@gti.net
www.tdi-dog.org

Training

Association of Pet Dog Trainers (APDT)
150 Executive Center Drive
Box 35
Greenville, SC 29615
Telephone: (800) PET-DOGS
Fax: (864) 331-0767
E-mail: information@apdt.com
www.apdt.com

Veterinary and Health Resources

American Animal Hospital Association (AAHA)
P.O. Box 150899
Denver, CO 80215-0899
Telephone: (303) 986-2800
Fax: (303) 986-1700
E-mail: info@aahanet.org
www.aahanet.org/index.cfm

American College of Veterinary Internal Medicine (ACVIM)
1997 Wadsworth Blvd., Suite A
Lakewood, CO 80214-5293
Telephone: (800) 245-9081
Fax: (303) 231-0880
Email: ACVIM@ACVIM.org
www.acvim.org

American College of Veterinary Ophthalmologists (ACVO)
P.O. Box 1311
Meridian, Idaho 83860
Telephone: (208) 466-7624
Fax: (208) 466-7693
E-mail: office@acvo.com
www.acvo.com

American Holistic Veterinary Medical Association (AHVMA)
2218 Old Emmorton Road
Bel Air, MD 21015

Telephone: (410) 569-0795
Fax: (410) 569-2346
E-mail: office@ahvma.org
www.ahvma.org

American Veterinary Medical Association (AVMA)
1931 North Meacham Road – Suite 100
Schaumburg, IL 60173
Telephone: (847) 925-8070
Fax: (847) 925-1329
E-mail: avmainfo@avma.org
www.avma.org

ASPCA Animal Poison Control Center
1717 South Philo Road, Suite 36
Urbana, IL 61802
Telephone: (888) 426-4435
www.aspca.org

Canine Eye Registration Foundation (CERF)
VMDB/CERF
1248 Lynn Hall
625 Harrison St.
Purdue University
West Lafayette, IN 47907-2026
Telephone: (765) 494-8179
E-mail: CERF@vmbd.org
www.vmdb.org

Orthopedic Foundation for Animals (OFA)
2300 NE Nifong Blvd
Columbus, Missouri 65201-3856
Telephone: (573) 442-0418
Fax: (573) 875-5073
Email: ofa@offa.org
www.offa.org

Note: Boldface numbers indicate illustrations; an italic *t* indicates tables.

mites, 95, 180–182
motels, dog-friendly, 60
motion sickness, 58
motivation, positive, 115, 116
mushrooms, 81

N
nail care, 96–97, **97**
names for Australian Shepherd, 11–12
National Association of Professional Pet Sitters, 62
neutering and spaying, 164–165
nighttime housetraining, 109
nipping, 38–39
noncommercial diets, 71–73, 83*t*
nuclear sclerosis, 174
nutrition, 65–69. *See also* feeding
Nylabone, 55, 57, 94, 133

O
obedience competition, 152–154, **152–153**
obedience training, 120–128
obesity, 76–79, 80
ocular dysgenesis, merle, 174–175
older dogs. *See* senior dogs
onions and garlic, 81
online dog purchases, 45
organizations and associations, 201–202
Orthopedic Foundation for Animals (OFA) certification, 50, 176
osteoarthritis, 176

P
pack behavior, 37, 38
papers, 49–51
parasites
    external, 180–184
    internal, 184–188
    protozoal, 188–189
    raw food and, 71
parvovirus, 168
pedigree and registration application, 51
periodontal disease, 91, 92, **95**
personality, 31–32, 114
pets
    Australian Shepherd and other, 36–37, **39**
    Australian Shepherd as, 32–33
pet sitters, 62, 63, 201
Pet Sitters International, 62
plaque and tartar, 91–92
play between dogs and kids, 39
Poison Control Hotline, 191, 192
poisoning, 81, 196

power of herding dog, 29–30
premium foods, 70

prescription diets, 73
preventive care, 163–164
problem behaviors. *See* behavior problems
progressive retinal atrophy (PRA), 175
prong collars, 52–53
proportion standards, 18, 27–28, **28**
propylene glycol, 70
protein in diet, 67–68
protein-sparing nutrients, 66
protozoal intestinal infections, 188–189
puppies
    adult dogs vs., 41–43
    certifications for, 51
    chewing by, 131–134, 135
    children and, 38
    choosing, 48
    crate training, 105–107
    exercise for, 35
    feeding, 72, 73–74, 78
    first exam for, 163
    grooming, 86
    Heimlich maneuver for, 193
    housetraining, 107–113, 114
    kindergarten for, 116
    leash training, 117–120
    obedience training, 121
    overweight, 80
    purchasing from breeders, 45, 46
    socialization of, 42, 101–105
    teeth/teething in, 24, 133
    temperament of, 31
    training methods for, 113–116
    vaccinations for, 165
puppy-proofing, 51, 52, 133

R
rabies, 168–169
raisins and grapes, 81, 134
rally obedience, 154
raw food and bones diet, 71–72, 83*t*
red merle, 22, **23**
registration, 14, **50**, 51
registries, 13–14, 46
reinforcement, positive, 116
release words, 123, 124, 125
rescue organizations, 48–49, 51, 201
resources, 201–202
retinal atrophy, progressive, 175
retinal dysplasia, 174, 175
retractable leads, 54
retrieving exercises, **152–153**
rewards in training, 80, 116, 120
rods and cones, 175
Romans, 6
roundworms, 186
running off, 139

S
safety
    home and yard, 51, 52, 133
    sports, 155
sales contract, 49–50
scheduled vs. free-feeding, 72
schedule for housetraining, 109–110
scissors bite, 24
Scotland, 7–8
Second Time Around Aussie Rescue, Inc. (STAAR), 51
seizures, 172–173
semi-moist food, 70, 83*t*
senior dogs
    exercise needs for, 36
    feeding, 74–76, 78
    health issues for, 164, 196–197
separation anxiety, 139
service dogs, 159
shaker cans, 130–131
shampoos and conditioners, 90–91
shaving, 88
shedding, 87
sheepdogs, 6, 7, 8, 9
sheepdog trials, 149
sheep industry, 7, 10
shelters, 49
shepherd-type dogs, 7, 10, 11
A Shepherd Watches, A Shepherd Sings (Irigaray), 20
showing. *See* conformation shows
Sisler's blue dogs, 13
Sit command, 122–123, **123**, 124
Sit-Stay command, 124–125, 126
size and proportion, 27–28
skijoring, 157
skin care, 85, 87–91
slicker burn, 89
snapping, 81
socialization, 42, 101–105
    early, 102
    problem behavior and, **138–139**
    tip for, 103
    training process for, 103–105
    your role in, 102–103
"soft" dog, 30
Sollosy, Paul, 11–12
Spain, 7, 11
spaying and neutering, 164–165
specialty shows, 147
sports. *See* training and activities, advanced
sports organizations, 201–202
"stacked" pose, **147**
Stay command, 124–125, 126
"sticky" dog, 29
stockdog program, ASCA's, 14, 149–151
stripping undercoat, 86
supplements, 67, 76, 189
Sweet Promised Land (Laxalt), 27

ACKNOWLEDGMENTS

My most grateful thanks to my husband, Paul, whose love and encouragement have been the constant in my life, enabling me to the opportunity to write and train dogs every day. Special thanks to Linda Rorem for her historical research and for unselfishly sharing her knowledge; C.A. Sharp for her genetic expertise and ongoing generosity; Louis Irigaray, and the relatives of Andrew Little and Dominque Laxalt for sharing their time, dog stories, and family heritage; Colin Sealy at the Kennel Club (UK); and all of the interesting and remarkable Aussie owners I have had the good fortune to meet the last twenty years. There have been so many that to mention them all would fill an entire book! A sincere thank you to Bobbie Anderson and Sylvia Bishop for their training, insight and words of wisdom through the years, and to Heather Russell-Revesz at TFH Publications, Inc., for her patience, intestinal fortitude, and guidance.
Finally, to all the Aussies, past and present, who have touched my life and who are the source and inspiration for this book. I live in gratitude to each and every one.

ABOUT THE AUTHOR

Tracy Libby is an award-winning freelance writer and coauthor of *Building Blocks for Performance* (Alpine 2002). Her articles have appeared in numerous publications, including the *AKC Gazette*, *Puppies USA*, *You and Your Dog*, and Dog Fancy's *Popular Dogs* series. She is a member of the Dog Writers Association of America and a recipient of the Ellsworth S. Howell award for distinguished dog writing. She lives in Oregon, and has been involved in the sport of dogs for 22 years, exhibiting Australian Shepherds in conformation and obedience.

PHOTO CREDITS

Mary Burlingame (Petscapes Animal Photography): 18, 30, 31, 33, 82 (top), 83 (bottom), 108, 134, 162, 170, 188, back cover top
Paul Clark (Bend Photography): 148
Cherlyn Evers: 89, 116
Hartnagle Archive: 9, 16, 19, 28, 58, 61, 102, 122, 130, 131, 147, 150, 151, 156, 167, 169, 175, 181, 185, 190, 192
Tracy Libby: 8, 11, 12, 15, 35, 37, 39, 44, 60, 79, 90, 95, 136, 138, 140, 142, 152, 154, 173, 180, 187, 197 (bottom)
Glen R. McLoughlin (Shutterstock): 113
Lynne Ouchida: 24, 49, 105, 171
Shannon Phifer: 6
April Turner (Shutterstock): 77

All other photos and cover photo courtesy Isabelle Francais

Nylabone® Cares.

Dogs of all ages, breeds, and sizes have enjoyed our world-famous chew bones for over 50 years. For the safest, healthiest, and happiest lifetime your dog can possibly have, choose from a variety of Nylabone® Pet Products!

Toys

Treats

Chews

Crates

Grooming

Available at retailers everywhere. Visit us online at www.nylabone.com